C0-AXB-839

Mystical Transformations

Mystical Transformations

The Imagery of Liquids
in the Work of
Mechthild von Magdeburg

James C. Franklin

Rutherford • Madison • Teaneck
Fairleigh Dickinson University Press
London: Associated University Presses

032896
0262674

© 1978 by Associated University Presses, Inc.

Associated University Presses, Inc.
Cranbury, New Jersey 08512

Associated University Presses
Magdalen House
136–148 Tooley Street
London SE1 2TT, England

Library of Congress Cataloging in Publication Data

Franklin, James C   1943–
Mystical transformations.

Bibliography: p. 172
Includes index.
1. Mechthild, of Magdeburg, ca. 1212–ca. 1282.
Das fliessende Licht der Gottheit. 2. Mysticism—

Middle Ages, 600–1500. I. Title.
BV5080.M333F7   282'.092'4   75–5248
ISBN 0-8386-1738-7

PRINTED IN THE UNITED STATES OF AMERICA

To Ruth Angress *and* Nancy Franklin

Contents

0262678
032896

Note from Author

Frequently in this book I have used collective nouns in the masculine gender, a practice that may seem particularly unfortunate in a book about the work of a woman poet. And I apologize to anyone who may be offended by this. However, at this time there is not yet a practical alternative that is neither clumsy nor confusing; perhaps there will be in the future.

032836

Acknowledgments

I want to thank Ruth Angress for her advice and encouragement, Ingeborg Hinderschiedt for her assistance with translation problems, Fairleigh Dickinson University Press for undertaking publication of my text, and the editors of Associated University Presses, Inc. for their assistance in revising the manuscript.

I also wish to thank the following publishers for having given me permission to quote from published works:

Cornell University Press, for permission to quote from Friedrich Solmsen: ARISTOTLE'S SYSTEM OF THE PHYSICAL WORLD. © 1960 by Cornell University.

Harvard University Press, for permission to quote from Arthur O. Lovejoy, *The Great Chain of Being, A Study of the History of an Idea*, 1966.

The Westminster Press, for permission to quote from CHRISTIANITY AND SYMBOLISM by F. W. Dillistone. Published 1955, The Westminster Press.

Introduction

Mechthild von Magdeburg, according to her own testimony in *Das fliessende Licht der Gottheit* or *The Flowing Light of the Divine,* experienced ecstatic visions from the age of twelve. Some thirty years later she began to record these experiences, and both her visions and her recording of them continued almost until the end of her life. This volume of revelations, written in Low German during the second half of the thirteenth century, comprises the entire canon of Mechthild von Magdeburg.

Divided into seven books of an unequal number of chapters of varying length and written in a rhythmic prose that frequently changes into verse, Mechthild's work is actually something more than a volume of revelations. In addition to descriptions of her visions, Mechthild's work contains allegorical tableaux, practical instructions for the everyday life of ecclesiastics, criticisms of the shortcomings of the Pope and the Church, and passages written to defend herself against the attacks of hostile critics. The division of *Das fliessende Licht* into seven books appears to be a delineation of seven creative periods of Mechthild's life rather than a device for structural organization, with the chronological progression of her work being reflected by changes of theme and imagery.

Mystical experience is generally held to be of two basic types: intuitive and speculative. Mechthild's mysticism, especially as found in the early books but even in the late ones, is intuitive; it is intensely personal and predominantly concerned with individual and immediate ecstatic experience of the divine. Unlike the work of Bernard of Clairvaux, before Mechthild, and that of Meister Eckhart, after her, Mechthild's work demonstrates little of the abstract, theoretical, philosophical characteristics of speculative mysticism. Mechthild's work stands near the beginning of a medieval religious and literary phenomenon known as *Frauenmystik* or *Nonnenmystik*. This phenomenon arose in the numerous convents and religious institutions founded for women during the twelfth and thirteenth centuries, particularly in northern Europe. Derivative in both thought and expression, much of the literature produced by these women is characterized by ecstatic effusiveness and by an often uninhibited eroticism. Mechthild's work, on the other hand, exhibits qualities of originality and restraint that give it a literary stature far above that attained by the work of most other visionaries of this era. Because of Mechthild's unique poetic ability, *Das fliessende Licht* is considered to be the first great literary work of German mysticism, which reached its peak in the speculative mysticism of Eckhart, Suso, and Tauler in the fourteenth century.

In 1869 P. Gall Morel published the first and, even today, the only modern edition of her work, an edition greatly flawed by misreadings and careless interpretations. Much of the subsequent Mechthild scholarship has thus been dedicated to correcting Gall Morel's errors.[1] In addition the details of Mechthild's biography, as is true with most medieval writers, are difficult to determine and a number of researchers have attempted to sort out what is known about her life and to hypothesize about what is not known.[2] Of the few studies dealing with Mechthild's work as literature, most have contented themselves with demonstrating influences of and analogies with other mystic writers rather than dealing with *Das fliessende Licht* as an independent and original work.[3] Only a few studies have attempted to investigate extensively any one aspect of Mechthild's work.[4] As a result, analyses of *Das fliessende Licht* as a unique and poetically creative work have been somewhat neglected. An investigation of Mechthild's symbolic language is necessary less because of its demonstration of any particular tradition or influence than because of its presence in a creative work. The mystical experience is one of the most highly personal experiences possible for man, and thus a literary recapitulation of mystical experience reflects this individuality. Mechthild employed traditional and contemporary ideas but molded them to her own purposes. In particular, she drew upon Hellenic scientific ideas and traditional Christian symbolism to create an individualized poetic and mystic system of elemental imagery.

There exists in *Das fliessende Licht* a general group of images based on the medieval concept of water and fluids as one of the four primary and irreducible elements that were thought to comprise the totality of matter within the cosmos. This group of images, each one related to the other by the primary characteristic of liquidity, has in Mechthild's work a number of specific symbolic meanings, these meanings arising not only from the physical properties of fluids but also from the significance traditionally ascribed, in the Bible and elsewhere, to water specifically and to liquids generally. Mechthild drew upon medieval science, mystical tradition, and Biblical precedent to create an individual symbolism of liquid substances as representations of divine grace and of the interaction of mystical love between God and man.

Notes to Introduction

1. *See*, for example, Hubert Stierling's "Studien zu Mechthild von Magdeburg" (Ph.D. dissertation, Göttingen, 1907); or Hans Neumann's "Problemata Mechtildiana," *Zeitschrift für deutsches Altertum und deutsche Literatur* 82 (1948/50): 143–72; or Neumann's "Beiträge zur Textgeschichte des 'Fliessenden Lichts der Gottheit' und zur Lebensgeschichte Mechthilds von Magdeburg" in *Altdeutsche und Altniederländische Mystik*, ed. Kurt Ruh (Darmstadt: Wissenschaftliche Buchgesellschaft, 1964), pp. 175–239.

2. Biographical information is found, for example, in Neumann's "Beiträge" and, most extensively, in Jeanne Ancelet-Hustache's thorough psychological study, *Mechtilde de Magdebourg (1207–1282), étude de psychologie religieuse* (Paris: Librairie Ancienne Honoré Champion, 1926).

3. Lothar Meyer's "Studien zur geistlichen Bildsprache im Werke der Mechthild von Magdeburg" (Ph.D. dissertation, Göttingen, 1951), for example, points out similarities between the mystical imagery of Mechthild and that of Bernard of Clairvaux; and Grete Lüers in *Die Sprache der deutschen Mystik des Mittelalters im Werke der Mechthild von Magdeburg* (Munich: Ernst Reinhardt Verlag, 1926) demonstrates the representativeness of Mechthild's poetic language for the mainstream of traditional Christian mysticism, in general, and of medieval German mysticism, specifically. This work will hereinafter be referred to as: Lüers.

4. Among the relatively few works that do examine specific themes are Hans Tillman's "Studien zum Dialog bei Mechthild von Magdeburg" (Ph.D. dissertation, Marburg, 1933); and Margot Schmidt's "Studien zum Leidproblem bei Mechthild von Magdeburg" (Ph.D. dissertation, Freiburg i. Br., 1952).

Orthographic peculiarities and inconsistencies of the original text as printed in Gall Morel's 1869 edition have been retained here. These should present no difficulties, with the possible exceptions of 1) "n̄" instead of "nn" and "m̄" instead of "mm" as in "min̄e" instead of "minne" and "benom̄en" instead of "benommen" and 2) the abbreviations "dc" instead of "das" and, less frequently, "wc" instead of "was."

Mystical Transformations

1

The Medieval System of
Four Primary Elements

A study of the history of philosophy and science reveals that
Germany and in fact all of Europe of the thirteenth century,
the era of Mechthild von Magdeburg, was a society in which
scientific theories were substantially identical with those that
had dominated Western thought since the time of Empedocles, Plato, and Aristotle. The reasons for this lack of
intellectual development lie, of course, in the nature of
medieval society itself: in its rural character, in its isolation,
in its domination by the Church of Rome. As can be seen
from the condemnations of Abelard, gained by Bernard of
Clairvaux in the twelth century, and much later from the
Inquisition's persecution of Galileo, the basic attitude of the
Church was that scientific investigation too often seemed to
be an attempt to call into question the ultimate truths of
God and his works. At one time during the thirteenth century the works of Aristotle were banned for nonecclesiastical
readers because of "a widespread phobia of Aristotelian
philosophy as tending towards determinism and a necessi-
tarian cosmology." [1] The Church's interference with the ad-

vancement of scientific knowledge was nowhere more apparent than in the natural sciences:

> During the Middle Ages those who pursued the natural sciences had no legitimate niche in society, nor were they recognized by the Church. The universities eschewed technical activities . . . as "illiberal arts," banishing them to the backrooms and workshops of small craftsmen and persons of dubious reputation. Theology frowned on any attempt at reaching into the secrets of nature, an unlawful invasion of the sacred womb of the Great Mother.[2]

Given this antagonism toward scientific investigation, it is not surprising that the attitudes of the thirteenth century concerning the universe and the elements should have been fundamentally the attitudes that had originated in the Hellenic world. Despite the short-lived official condemnation of Aristotle's thought, his work and that of Empedocles, Plato,[3] and others were well known among educated people. The basic ideas of the Greek philosophers concerning the composition of the natural world seem to have become a matter of common knowledge and to have been accepted insofar as they did not interfere with the philosophical and religious dogma of the Church. Neoplatonic-Aristotelian scientific ideas and Christian theological concepts were then synthesized by medieval philosophers, a synthesis exemplified by Thomas Aquinas's writings during Mechthild's lifetime.

According to the scientific beliefs prevalent in the Middle Ages, the universe was composed of four primal elements: earth, water, air, and fire. According to this theory, which had originated in the fifth century B.C. in the philosophy of Empedocles, these four elements, standing either alone or in combination with one or more of the others, were the ultimate and irreducible components of everything that exists within the universe, from a grain of sand to man to the clouds and stars. It has been said that with this theory Empedocles became

> the founder of one of the most gigantic theoretical syntheses in the history of science. It remained the leading working hypothesis until the sixteenth century and even until the beginning of the seventeenth.[4]

Related to Empedocles' theory of the four elements was the theory of the four humors of the human body—blood, phlegm, yellow bile, and black bile—by which man, the microcosm, reflects the universe, the macrocosm. These theories of four elements and four humors were modified to some extent by later philosophers, including Plato, Aristotle, and Galen, but essentially this view of the composition of man, earth, and the universe endured until the end of the Middle Ages.

The Neoplatonists used Empedocles' theory of fundamental elements to formulate a cosmology in which three celestial spheres, corresponding to the nonearth elements—water, air, and fire—were thought to encircle earth, the terrestrial sphere. These spheres were concentric, becoming larger as they became more distant from earth:

> their sizes relative to that of the earth (radius=1) were: water 2, air 5, and fire 10, the nearest round cubes of 1, 10, 100, and 1,000. The first three layers constituted the sublunary world, while the fourth, fire, contained the stars.[5]

The Neoplatonic cosmology, like Empedocles' theory of elements, remained relatively unchanged until the Renaissance.

These Hellenic ideas were adapted by medieval Christians to correspond to contemporary theological theory. A good example, for the purpose of a study of Mechthild, of this adaptational tendency is demonstrated by the cosmology of Hildegard von Bingen, a German mystic of the twelfth century, as this cosmology was described in her Latin works of revelations and theological theorizing, *Scivias, Liber Divinorum Operum Simplicis Hominis,* and *Liber Vitae Meritorum.* Although Hildegard lived a century before Mechthild and was without question a more educated woman, the abundant similarities of their situations would seem to justify using Hildegard's ideas as a very general indication of Mechthild's own thought. Both were attached to convents—Hildegard as a Benedictine nun, Mechthild as a Dominican Beguine; both came from similarly privileged-aristocratic backgrounds; both exhibited a predisposition toward ecstatic mysticism coupled with creative talents that enabled them to convey their experiences to their contemporaries. Because of the similarity of their backgrounds and lives and because of the exceedingly slow pace of advancement in scientific thought during the Middle Ages, it seems safe to assume that the ideas of both women concerning the natural sciences would be generally similar.

According to Hildegard, the cosmos, like the cosmos of Aristotle and the Neoplatonists, consisted of four concentric spheres, each sphere corresponding to one of the four fundamental elements; and the cosmos as a whole was contained within and controlled by the Christian godhead. The four elemental spheres of Hildegard's cosmology ascended upward toward God according to loss of density, with earth, the realm of men and the terrestrial world, lying below the spheres of water, air, and fire. Fire, being the least dense, was the realm of the stars and the elemental sphere lying closest to God.[6] The concept of elemental spheres formed by the relative densities of the four elements had originated

with Aristotle, who had characterized the elements according
to the four qualities—cold, hot, dry, and moist:

> [Aristotle] builds up the four elements in such a way as to
> give the "equations": cold+dry=earth, cold+moist=
> water, hot+moist=air, hot+dry=fire. The first two equa-
> tions produce the quality "heavy" which is the opposite
> of the quality "light" produced by the other two.[7]

Just as essentially Hellenic elemental and cosmological
theories are found in adapted form in the works of Hildegard von Bingen, so do they form a basis for the ideas that
underlie the imagery of Mechthild von Magdeburg's *Das
fliessende Licht der Gottheit*.

Mechthild's Use of the Four-Element System

Mechthild's belief in the Hellenic theory of elements
must be inferred from her work and from the ideas of her
contemporaries because, unlike Hildegard von Bingen,
Mechthild at no time attempted to systematize or define her
own scientific beliefs. Mechthild was, as she herself emphasized, relatively uneducated: "Nu gebristet mir túsches,
des latines kan ich nit, so was hie gûtes anliget, das ist min
schult nit, ..."[8] From what is known of Mechthild's life,
it would appear that, in all probability, her profession of
ignorance is more than a merely rhetorical disclaimer. Her
position as a Beguine in a Dominican convent indicates that
Mechthild was of aristocratic origin, was wealthy enough to
provide her own support, was sufficiently educated to write
down her visions, but still not so educated that her book
could have been written in Latin, which would have been
the more respectable and thus preferred language for a
religious work. The effect of this relative lack of education
in medieval convents can be demonstrated by the fact that

many of Meister Eckhart's sermons were given in German, rather than Latin, simply because they were intended for the elucidation of the nuns and Beguines of the convents in his charge. Even Mechthild's limited education would have made her aware, although perhaps only superficially, of the Hellenic elemental and cosmological theories. This knowledge is one foundation for much of the imagery that she employed in her book of revelations.

The hypothesis that the concept of four primal elements underlies the poetic thought in Mechthild's work is further supported by the work of the twentieth-century French literary critic, Gaston Bachelard. Bachelard, in studies such as *La Psychanalyse du Feu* and *L'eau et les Rêves. Essai sur l'imagination de la matière,* has shown that "la loi des quatre éléments poétiques" ("the law of four poetic elements") serves as a basis for poetic thought, not only through the Middle Ages and the Renaissance, but also in the literature of the nineteenth and twentieth centuries. Drawing convincing examples from Goethe, Novalis, Tieck, the English Romantics, Poe, the French Symbolists, and even Nietzsche and T. S. Eliot, Bachelard maintains that even in an age that denies the validity of a universe composed of four elements, there exists in the collective poetic unconscious a belief in such a four-element system:

> En effet, nous croyons possible de fixer, dans le règne de l'imagination, une loi des quatre éléments qui classe les diverses imaginations matérielles suivant qu'elles s'attachent au feu, à l'air, à l'eau ou à la terre.[9]

Bachelard demonstrates that even in the works of a poet who would consciously deny the existence of a four-element system, there can be found patterns of imagery that conform to such a system. If one can accept Bachelard's assertions about modern poets, it becomes easier to accept a similar assertion about the work of a poet who would probably have consciously affirmed these ideas, as it is in the case of Mechthild von Magdeburg.

Theoretically, according to the medieval concept of the universe, the four spheres of earth, water, air, and fire define the world of man and the area between man and God but in no way are representative of God himself. The godhead and heaven lie beyond the furthest limits of the known universe, that is, beyond the sphere of fire, the realm of the stars. Various theories were developed that attempted to describe the realm of God, but there was no unanimity of opinion as there had been in considerations of the cosmos containing the earth and the stars. Thus, it is unlikely that Mechthild would have been provided with any credible, quasi-scientific explanation of the nature of this realm. Because of this, probably, Mechthild was led to describe her God, His actions, and His love for the human soul in terms of the terrestrial elements.

The representation of an ineffable divinity is, to be sure, an essential problem of all mystical writers, and Mechthild was no exception. This problem is normally considered to be caused by the inherent limitations of language. A mystic writer is eternally confronted with the impossibility of describing something that is fundamentally indescribable, of expressing the inexpressible, of defining the indefinable : "dc allerliebste mûs ich verswigen" ("About the dearest and the best I must remain silent") (p. 221). Grete Lüers has shown that this problem was not only Mechthild's, but is also commonplace with most mystical writings :

> Immer wieder kommt das Bekenntnis des Nicht-reden-
> könnens und Schweigen-müssens gerade in den Augen-
> blicken, . . . wenn die göttlich Minnende der innigsten
> Einung mit dem Geliebten teilhaftig ward.[10]

At the same time, this striving for the impossible is responsible for the importance of the German mystics for the
historical development of the German language. By word
coinings, word combinations, translations of Latin terminology, and the extension of word meanings, the mystics expanded the capacity of German for use as a philosophical
and literary language. Just as the mystic writer is forced to
use a language limited in its capacity for expression, so is
he also forced to use his own environment, the world of
man, as a source for images to represent a divinity who
stands outside that environment. In this way, Mechthild von
Magdeburg in *Das fliessende Licht der Gottheit* drew upon
her own environment in order to find images for her experience of God. And just as the Empedoclean theory of four
elements underlies much of the scientific thought of the
Middle Ages, so too does it form a most basic characteristic
in the imagery of Mechthild's work. Viewed in this way, the
imagery in her work can be divided into elemental groups :
images of earth, water, air, and fire, each group having its
own peculiarities and significance.

Although this study will examine at length only the
imagery of water and liquids and investigate briefly the
significance of the imagery of earth and solids, further study
would reveal the existence of well-developed image groups
relating to all four elements. Water and liquids, because of
their associations in the Bible and in Christian tradition
generally and because of their unique properties, have a
central importance for Mechthild's imagery. Earth and
solids, because of their identification with the earthly exis-

tence of man and because of Mechthild's religious beliefs, also are significant. The thematic content of her work, that is, the existence of man on earth and the interaction of man and God, is primarily responsible for a predominance of water and earth imagery, with the imagery of air and fire being of secondary importance in *Das fliessende Licht*. Mechthild was, for the most part, not an overly logical or consciously theoretical writer, and it may be that she was herself unaware of the patterns to be found in her imagery. A close investigation of the specific images employed and their significance within the context of the entire work, nevertheless, makes it abundantly clear that such patterns do exist.

Because the Empedoclean principle was an inclusion of all things that exist, all the material images in Mechthild's work can be interpreted as fitting into one or more of the four elemental groups. Viewed within this framework, new relationships and significances become apparent that are not always explainable if each specific image is considered to stand alone. For example, the loving human soul is described in one passage in *Das fliessende Licht* as a sick child, as a needy friend, as a repentant sinner, as a sister, as a beloved daughter, as a hungry traveler, and as a bride (pp. 248–49). Obviously the basic conception of the loving soul in its relationship to God is not specifically any of these images; it is rather *all* of them. In a sense, the ultimate meaning of the many specific images is not even merely the total of these images; it is rather a transcendence of them all; that is, the whole is greater than the sum of the parts. This type of transcendent significance seems to be characteristic of the majority of Mechthild's images and can be appreciated only by an examination according to general image groups, such as those of the four elements.

Mechthild's Avoidance of Earth Imagery
in Descriptions of the Divine

One of the most striking examples of the elemental image groups found in Mechthild's work is evident in the descriptions of the Trinity and its manifestations. In any work of this nature—that is, a book of mystical revelations—there are innumerable references to God, Christ, and the Holy Spirit. What is notable is Mechthild's almost total avoidance of solid imagery or imagery employing substances of the earth in her references to the Trinity. Clearly, according to medieval thought, God would have been considered the creator of *all* the elements and, although no element could represent the total essence of God, it might seem strange that any one element would be considered totally unrepresentative of God. From the uses of earth imagery throughout Mechthild's work, however, it becomes clear that earth substances are almost never employed to describe the Trinity because of their close identification with the flesh of man, with transience, with sinfulness and evil. These attributes being the opposite of Mechthild's concept of the attributes of the Trinity, the justification for the avoidance of earth images becomes very obvious. The Trinity is, on the other hand, represented through the three remaining element groups: water, air, and fire.

In general, many of Mechthild's representations of the Trinity are derivative and merely indicate the strong influence of precedent and tradition, as Grete Lüers has convincingly demonstrated in her book about *Das fliessende Licht*. The use that Mechthild made of many of these traditional images is, however, less attributable to tradition. For example, the representation of God as the sun, as a distant but perceptible giver of light and warmth, is one of the most common of traditional mystic images; Mecht-

032896

hild's employment of this image is less clearly the result of precedent. In the last book of *Das fliessende Licht* the effect of God upon the human soul is described as the effect of the sun upon the air:

> Dc gehúgenisse gotz und der miñenden sele kumet zesamene glicherwis als dú suñe und der luft mit der edelen gotzkraft sich zesañene menget in einem sůssen gedrenge, dc die suñe dem luft sin keltnisse und vinsternisse v́berwindet. (p. 269)

> The thoughts of God and of the loving soul come together just as the sun and the air are mingled by the power of God in one sweet union so that the sun overcomes the air's coldness and darkness.

Although traditional images were employed by Mechthild, they were added to or changed by the context in which they were employed. Moreover, in spite of the acknowledged influence of tradition, this influence alone does not explain the almost complete avoidance of earth images to describe God. This omission is made all the more striking in a passage, such as the following, in which God is described through three images, each one of which represents one of the nonearth elements. Here, in a dialogue between the soul and the senses, the soul explains how she is able to bear the unbearable power of God within the *unio mystica:*

> Der visch mag in dem wasser nit ertrinken,
> Der vogel in dem lufte nit versinken.
> Das gold mag in dem fúre nit verderben,
> Wan es enpfât da sin klarheit und sin lúhtende varwe.
>
> (p. 21)

> The fish can not drown in the water,
> The bird can not sink in the air,
> Gold can not perish in the fire,
> For it finds there its pure beauty and its glowing color.

Related to this combining of the three nonearth elements to create images of God is Mechthild's paradoxical linking of two elemental attributes within one image. Here again, any combination of water, air, and fire seems possible, but earth metaphors are completely avoided. The most striking example of this paradoxical combining of elemental attributes is seen in the title of Mechthild's work in which *fliessen,* an attribute of water, is applied to the word *Licht,* an attribute of fire. Similarly the love of God for the soul is described as a flowing fire ("mit dem vliessenden fúre der gôtlichen miñe" ["with the flowing fire of divine love"] [p. 129]), combining the elemental realms of fire and water. The juxtaposing of images of the three nonearth elements and the paradoxical combining of two elemental attributes have a double effect within Mechthild's work: first of all, to emphasize the exclusion of earth imagery in descriptions of the divine and, second, to illustrate the transcendence of God over the limitations of any one elemental realm. God may be found in water or air or fire, but He can not be contained within any or all of them.

Transition and Tangibility as Bases for Water Imagery in Mechthild's Work

In spite of Mechthild's use of images of air and fire to describe God, there is an unmistakable preponderance of imagery in *Das fliessende Licht* that portrays the Trinity, its manifestations, the loving soul, and, most important, the love of God and the soul as water substances. The concept of water as one of the four elements includes not only water itself but also any fluid, such as blood, wine, milk, tears, and any other substance of which the primary characteristic would be liquidity. The characterization of God, of spirituality, and of the love relationship between God and man as

⌒262678

being liquid is arbitrary, although certain justifications for such a tendency in a medieval writer can be determined. Most simply and, perhaps for Mechthild, most fundamentally this employment of water imagery would have to bear some relation to the general beliefs of the poet and would thus have to possess some attribute that would make it preferable to the other three elements. As has been mentioned before, earth imagery would not have been used in descriptions of the divine because of the close identification of earth with the flesh of man and with evil. Less obvious, however, is why liquid or water imagery should predominate over images of air and fire.

One possible explanation is that, as J. E. Cirlot has written, "water is of all the elements, the most clearly transitional, between fire and air (the ethereal elements) and earth (the solid element)." [11] Accordingly, for Mechthild, that which is fluid, of the sphere of water, signified the possibility for contact between God and man. Man is tied to the earth and solidity and can not attain the ethereal spheres of air and fire; God, on the other hand, only infrequently manifests himself as earth or solidity because of the attendant impurity and evil. Water is, by elimination of the other three elemental spheres, the only sphere simultaneously approachable for both God and man.

Related to the idea of water as the transitional element, moreover, is the idea that, other than earth, water is the most tangible of the elements. The mystic writer is constantly concerned with the apprehension of God, with grasping and holding the intangible; and within the *unio mystica,* the mystic believes that he actually does so. Thus, the ideal mystic image for God would be one that could demonstrate the tangibility of God for the loving soul. God can approach the soul within any one of the three nonearth spheres, but only as water can He literally be touched by man. Keeping in mind the cosmology of Hildegard von Bingen, the sphere of water is that which lies closest to the earth; it is water that is closest to man and the earth without bearing the taint of earthly substances.

Mechthild's striving for tangible images to express her intangible experiencing of God is a recurring characteristic of her work and indeed of most mystical literature. It is seen in various forms: in her use of water imagery, in her apparent obsession with tactile and physical sensation within the mystical experience (for example, the physical eroticism in descriptions of the *unio mystica* and the eating, drinking, and handling of God by man in the Eucharist and within the mystical union), and in the constant emphasis on the anatomy of God.[12] Mechthild's God, unlike the God of some other mystic writers, is actually thought to possess a perceivable countenance. He is "seen" not merely through his reflection upon earthly objects but as himself. One might suppose that if man was created in the image of God then God must be anatomically similar to man. Thus, Mechthild's God has not only a general countenance, but also eyes, ears, a mouth, arms and legs, feet, a chest, and a heart: "min gôtlich herze" ("my divine heart") (p. 18), "die grosse zunge der gotheit" ("the great voice of the divine") (p. 28), "ateme sines vliessenden mundes" ("breath of His flowing mouth") (p. 28), "so nim ich dich an den aren min" ("then I will take you in My arms") (p. 34), "sin vetterliche hant" ("His fatherly hand") (p. 56), and so forth.

This emphasis on sensory experiencing of God may be assumed to have its origins in Mechthild's total concept of the essence of man as a dual being, containing within himself both good and evil, both spirit and flesh. Man is bound to the earth and in many ways his experience is limited by his senses. Thus man must have a tangible God, an idea that found its logical and ideal fulfillment in the concept of Christ—God become man and the perfect union of spirit and flesh. It is important to note, however, that the body of Christ is untainted flesh, a concept that Mechthild frequently symbolized not through earth imagery but rather through images of water, which is tangible but not bound to or of the earth. Although other reasons can be given as justification for the prevalence of liquid or water imagery in Mechthild's *Das fliessende Licht der Gottheit*, as will be discussed later, the transitional quality of the element water, the mixture of tangibility and intangibility as a characteristic of liquids, and the traditional Biblical significance of liquids seem most responsible for Mechthild's reliance on this imagery.

Notes to Chapter 1

1. David Knowles, *The Evolution of Medieval Thought* (New York: Random House and Vintage Books, 1962), p. 300.

2. Friedrich Heer, *The Medieval World*, trans. Janet Sondheimer (New York and Toronto: Mentor Books and The New American Library, Inc., 1962), p. 293.

3. As interpreted by Plotinus and the Neoplatonists.

4. Abel Rey quoted in *History of Science*, Volume 1: *Ancient and Medieval Science*, ed. René Taton and tr. A. J. Pomerans (New York: Basic Books, Inc., 1963), p. 197.

5. Taton, *History of Science*, p. 226.

6. Charles Singer, "The Visions of Hildegard von Bingen" in *From Magic to Science* (New York: Boni and Liveright, 1928), pp. 199–239.

7. Samuel Sambursky, *The Physical World of the Greeks*, trans. Merton Dagut (New York: The Macmillan Company, 1956), p. 91.

8. *Offenbarungen der Schwester Mechthild von Magdeburg oder Das fliessende Licht der Gottheit*, ed. P. Gall Morel (Regensburg: 1869; reprint, Darmstadt: Wissenschaftliche Buchgesellschaft, 1963), p. 30. All further citations will be identified by the page number of the reprinted edition in this volume. "My German is lacking; I do not know Latin; so whatever good appears here is not owing to me."

9. Gaston Bachelard, *L'eau et les Rêves. Essai sur l'imagination de la matière* (Paris: Librairie José Corti, 1942), p. 4. "Indeed, we believe it

possible to determine, in the realm of the imagination, a law of four elements which classify the various imaginings of a material nature according to whether they refer to fire, to air, to water, or to earth."

10. Lüers, p. 6. "Again and again comes the admission of not-being-able-to-speak and of having-to-stay-silent precisely at those moments . . . when the divinely loving soul experienced the most fervent union with the Beloved."

11. J. E. Cirlot, A *Dictionary of Symbols* (New York: Philosophical Library, 1962), p. 345.

12. For a complete discussion of the importance of sensory imagery in the works of Meister Eckhart, *see* Peter Ober, "Sense Images for Noetic Experience in the Works of Meister Eckhart" (Ph.D. dissertation, University of California at Berkeley, 1968).

2

The Derogation of Earth Substances in *Das fliessende Licht*

One of Mechthild's primary concerns within *Das fliessende Licht der Gottheit* and especially within the later books of this work was the depiction of her conception of man's existence on earth. Most basically she considered the human soul to be trapped within the human body, an entrapment that could be ended permanently by the death of the body or temporarily within the *unio mystica*. The Middle Ages viewed man as a dual entity containing within himself two totally opposing and eternally incompatible essences: spirit and flesh. In order to comprehend the significance of Mechthild's concept of the soul, it is necessary to investigate not only the qualities of man's flesh or body as conveyed by means of earth imagery, but also the implications of earth imagery in general.

The Medieval Concept of the Great Chain of Being

In his book, *The Great Chain of Being*, Arthur O. Lovejoy states that medieval Christian Europe believed in a universal order in which all things were assigned a value according to their status on a scale ascending from utterly inanimate objects to plants and animals, to man, to the angels, and ultimately to God:

> The result of Aristotle's thought was the conception of the plan and structure of the world which, through the Middle Ages and down to the late eighteenth century, many philosophers, most men of science, and, indeed, most educated men were to accept without question— the conception of the universe as a "Great Chain of Being," composed of an immense . . . number of links ranging in hierarchical order from the meagerest kind of existents, which barely escape non-existence, through "every possible" grade up to the *ens perfectissimum* . . . every one of them differing from that immediately above and that immediately below it by the "least possible" degree of difference.[1]

According to this concept, which Lovejoy refers to as "the conception of the creation as a ladder for man's ascent," [2] the chain of being was not just a "chain" but also a "ladder"; and all forms of being were granted a potential for moving upward on the ladder. Because of this potential, the higher forms of one existential level would be quite similar to the lower forms of the next higher level. This belief pertained both to forms of being and to the elemental spheres. Each sphere touched upon and had a certain similarity to the spheres immediately above and below it. Thus, according to Aristotelian and medieval thought, there existed a possibility for transitions between the various elemental spheres:

> the elements have a common source and can change into each other: "We maintain that fire, air, water, and earth are transformable one into another, and that each is potentially latent in the others, as is true of all other things that have a single common substratum underlying them into which they can in the last resort be resolved." [3]

Bearing in mind the cosmology of Hildegard von Bingen, one would thus expect to perceive a similarity between the higher manifestations of earth and the lesser manifestations of water, between the higher manifestations of water and the lesser manifestations of air, and so on to the purest form of fire, which would be the sun and the most perfect elemental representation of God. In general this linking of elemental spheres can also be found in *Das fliessende Licht*, especially regarding the distinctions made between the various forms of water, as will be discussed later. Between the spheres of earth and water there existed, moreover, an overlapping of qualities between the lesser forms of water and the purer forms of earth: since water could be tainted by the earth, so could earth be purified by water. Simultaneously, however, it is important to remember that Mechthild considered man to be a being composed of two completely antithetical essences, spirit and flesh. She believed not only in a gradualistic universe but also in a universe dominated by antitheses and polarities, by oppositions that could be overcome by love alone and, specifically, by the love of God and the human soul.

This paradoxical concept of man and the universe as being simultaneously gradualistic and antithetical is reflected in Mechthild's imagery of the elements. Traditionally water is thought to have been the transitional element between the ethereal elements—air and fire—and the terrestrial element—earth. Mechthild, too, used water and liquids as symbols of transition between man's soul and his body, and between heaven—the realm of God—and earth—the realm of man. It is interesting to note at this point that Mechthild's contemporary Thomas Aquinas believed that man himself served as a transitional link in the chain of being, just as water serves as a transitional link between the ethereal elements and earth:

The material, the *genus corporum,* at its highest, namely, in man, passes over into the mental. Man's constitution is *"aequaliter complexionatum,* has in equal degree the character of both classes, since it attains to the lowest member of the class above bodies, namely, the human soul, which is at the bottom of the series of intellectual beings—and is said, therefore, to be the horizon and boundary line of things corporeal and incorporeal." [4]

It is precisely this unique position of man in the chain of being that dominates much of Mechthild's thought and indeed the thought of many medieval writers. For Mechthild, man was the "horizon and boundary line" not only of "things corporeal and incorporeal" but also, and more importantly, of evil and good, of flesh and spirit, of earth and heaven, of mortal and divine. One part of man's being, the incorporeal or spiritual, was infinitely preferable to the other, and Mechthild's greatest concern was man's transition from his body to his spirit. That such a transition was possible was implied both by the Aristotelian concept of the elements and by the Christian tradition. In *Das fliessende Licht* imagery of earth and water was employed to demonstrate this transition.

The Opposition of Spirit and Flesh

In distinct contrast with the ideals embodied within the medieval German concept of "hôhe minne," according to which material wealth and physical beauty are reflections of internal, spiritual virtue, there is in Mechthild's work a total separation of the qualities of body and soul. For Mechthild, the primary characteristic of the body was its impurity. Flesh itself might not be necessarily evil— in fact, seems not to have been evil before the expulsion of Adam and Eve from the Garden of Eden. Impurity, however, clings to the flesh of man; and this impurity can be avoided only by a denial and subjugation of the body.

The body and soul of man are two completely unrelated essences dwelling in man, and Mechthild consistently emphasized the disrelatedness of the two. Rather than harming the soul, suffering of the body leaves the soul untouched: "Tût ir das vleisch einen wank, / Davon wirt der geist nút krank" ("If the flesh does her [the soul] harm, / The spirit does not suffer from it") (p. 9). And conversely what is good for the soul—that is, the love of God—is a punishment for the body:

> Ich danke herre, dir diner súnlichen gaben, da du mich mitte rûrest ane vnderlas, die alles min gebein und alle min adern und alles min vleisch dursnidet. (pp. 264–65)

> I thank You, Lord, for all Your gifts with which You touch me without pause and which cut through all my bones and all my veins and all my flesh.

In this way man, being composed of both flesh and spirit, is a microcosm of the universal antithesis of evil and good; and it is man's free will that permits him to choose between the warring aspects of his own being. In *Das fliessende Licht* the concept of free will was exemplified for Mechthild as man's need for love. By his nature, man can and must love something but the love object is a matter of free choice. If man chooses wisely, he will select God; if unwisely, then he will select a transient love object such as material possessions, earthly power, or the love of another human being: "Die ewig liebi ze gotte wonot in der sele, / Die vergenglich liebi ze irdenschen dingen, die wonot in dem vleische" ("The eternal love for God resides in the soul, / The transient love for earthly things resides in the flesh")

(p. 260). If man chooses the love of God, the spiritual aspect
of his being becomes dominant; if, however, he chooses a
love of transient things, his flesh becomes dominant and
eternal salvation is forfeited. This opposition of soul and
body is nowhere made more obvious than in a dialogue
between the soul and the body in the first book of *Das
fliessende Licht*. Here the soul is scolded by the body because of the soul's absence from the body during the *unio
mystica*, and the domination of the soul over the body is
emphasized by the words assigned to each:

> So spricht der licham zu der sele:
> Wa bist du gewesen? Ich mag nit me.
> So spricht die sele: Swig, du bist ein tore.
> Ich wil mit mime liebe wesen,
> Soltest du niemer me genesen.

(p. 8)

> Thus the body speaks to the soul:
> Where have you been? I can bear it no longer.
> Thus speaks the soul: Be silent, you are a fool.
> I want to be with my love,
> Even if you should never recover.

Earth Images as Symbols of Impurity and Evil

More frequently, although perhaps less explicitly than
in such a dialogue, Mechthild demonstrated by means of
earth images her belief in the necessity for the subjugation
of the body. In a metaphor in which the human soul is
described as a keg that must be filled, the personification of
love ("Miñe") says that the natural function of the soul
("vas") is to be filled with the love of God ("win"), but a
perverted soul comes to be filled with the stones and ashes
of terrestrial things:

Was hilfet, das man ein ital vas vil bindet,
Und das der win doch usriñet?
So mûs man es fúllen mit Steinen der vswendigen arbeit
Und mit eschen der vergenglichkeit.

(p. 44)

What good does it do to bind an empty keg
If the wine still runs out?
Then it must be filled with stones of external works
And with ashes of transience.

Similarly at another point Mechthild represents the cardinal sins as stones:

Ich habe gesehen ein stat,
Ir name ist der ewige hass.
Si ist gebuwen in dem nidersten abgrunde
Von manigerlei steine der hŏptsúnden.
Die hoffart war der erste stein,
Als es an lucifer ist wol schein.

(p. 82)

I have seen a place,
Its name is eternal hatred.
It is built in the lowest abyss
From the stones of mortal sins.
Pride was the first stone,
As was seen in Lucifer.

and these stones must be eaten by souls in hell who hunger for God: "Die . . . essent glúiendige steine" ("They . . . eat glowing stones") (p. 84).

Although the soul and the body are polar essences, on earth one can not exist without the other and the actions of one necessarily affect the other. If the soul becomes

dominant, the body suffers, and vice versa. As the overindulgence of the body causes the soul to lose sight of God,
so is the love of the soul for God detrimental to the body.
In this way the *unio mystica,* the complete submission to
the desires of the soul, destroys the vitality of the body:
"Der ware gottes grûs . . . hat so grosse kraft, das er dem
lichamen benimet alle sine maht, . . ." ("The true greeting
of God . . . has such power that it takes all strength from
the body, . . .") (p. 4). Just as the soul may affect the body,
so can the demands of the body serve as a debilitation and
a tainting of the soul and its will to God. It is this tainting
of the free will of the soul that emphasizes the inferiority
of man to God: "Gotz wille ist luter, vnser wille ist sere
gemenget mit dem vleische" ("God's will is pure / Our will
is very mingled with the flesh") (p. 247). Showing the influence of Bernard of Clairvaux, Mechthild seemed to imply
that at times the tainting of the soul by the flesh is less a
question of a wrong choice by man's will than it is the in-
evitable result of the proximity of the soul and the flesh.
Thus a vision is described of the torments in purgatory of
priests whose souls were blinded by their flesh: "Dc fleisch
hatte verblendet iren geist, darumbe sutten si allermeist"
("The flesh had blinded their spirit; for this they simmered
the most") (p. 77). The priests seem to be punished less for
any overtly sinful action than for an inherent weakness
caused by the entrapment of the soul within the body. The
body is flesh; impurity clings to the flesh: "Swacheit des
lichamen kunt von dem vleisch alleine" ("Weakness of the
body comes from the flesh alone") (p. 37). Therefore, simply
because the soul is bound to the body, the soul is innately
corrupted to a certain degree (original sin). Because of this
tainting by the flesh, the soul can perceive God's truth only
through the subjugation and transcendence of the body:

Das man mit vleischlichen ôgen mag gesehen, mit vleischlichen oren mag gehôren, mit vleischlichem munde mag
gesprechen, dc ist also vngelich der offenen warheit der
miñenden sele, als ein wachslieht der claren sunen. (p. 210)

What one can see with eyes of flesh, can hear with ears of
flesh, can speak with mouth of flesh is as unlike the truth
revealed to the loving soul as a candle is to the shining
sun.

The identification of the corruption of the flesh with the
concept of original sin is repeatedly emphasized by Mechthild. In a passage describing the creation of Adam and Eve
and their expulsion from the Garden of Eden, the contrasting
symbolism of water and earth imagery is reinforced by the
use of the word *wasser* as a simile for man's flesh before the
Fall:

Ire [Adam and Eve's] lichamen sollen reine wesen, wan
got schûf inen nie schemeliche lide, und si waren gekleidet
mit engelscher wete. Ire kint sollen si gewiñen in heliger
miñe, als die suñe spilende in dc wasser schinet und doch
dc wasser vnzerbrochen blibet. Mere da si assen die ver-
botenen spise, do wurden si schemlich verschaffen an dem
libe, als es uns noch anschinet. (pp. 69–70)

Their bodies were to be pure, for God created nothing
to shame them, and they were clothed in angelic clothing.
Their children they were to conceive in holy love, as the
sun shines into the water and yet leaves the water undis-
turbed. But when they ate the forbidden food, their
bodies were shamefully transformed as is still apparent in
us.

The flesh of man before the Fall is equated with water; it
is only after the Fall that flesh became identified with impurity, transience, and grossness. After the Fall the body

or flesh of man was of the earth and bound to it. The body can have not part in the union of man and God; it is a union that can occur only in the spiritual realm because of the irradicable corruption of the flesh brought upon all mankind by the sin of Adam and Eve.

In spite of the corruption of the body, Mechthild, in keeping with the dogma of the Church, did foresee a resurrection of the body after the Last Judgment. At the same time, however, she apparently considered a resurrection of the physical body of man to be a miracle tantamount to the birth of Christ; and it was only through Christ that this resurrection of the body could be accomplished. The love of Christ for man is so all encompassing that it includes within its scope not only the soul but even the impure body of man. In a vision of the reception of loving souls in heaven, Mechthild wrote:

> Die menscheit vnsers herren grůsset,
> Vrǒwet und miñet ane vnderlas
> Sin [man's] vleisch und sin blůt.
> Alleine da vleisch noch blůt nu nit si,
> So ist doch die brůderliche sibbe also gros,
> Dc er sine menschlich nature
> Sunderlichen miñen můs.

(p. 219)

> The humanity of our Lord greets,
> Rejoices, and loves without ceasing
> His flesh and His blood.
> For, though flesh and blood now are no more,
> The brotherly relationship is so great
> That He must love especially
> His human nature.

Precisely because Christ is God become man, he is able to love all of man, body as well as soul. It is the ultimate miracle of Christ that makes possible the eventual resurrection of the body.

Representations of God and the Soul as Purified Earth Images

Flesh and the human body are considered in *Das fliessende Licht* to be earth substances. They are solid substances; and, when they are presented through images, earth images are used. They are specific manifestations of the general derogation of solid or earth substances throughout Mechthild's work. In general anything in *Das fliessende Licht* that is solid is related to the element earth and is therefore also related to evil, sinfulness, impurity, and transience. Just as the human body can attain resurrection through the miraculous love of Christ, however, there is a limited number of other solid substances that—through transformations effected, ultimately, by the love of God for the soul—can be raised to a level higher than the extreme baseness normally associated with earth.

Probably the most obvious, because it is the most prevalent, of these "purified earth" images are solid images that are at times applied both to the human body and to the soul. The soul is sometimes represented as a container for the love of God, and on a lower elemental plane the body is represented as a container for the soul. In both instances the container is improved by being filled. The soul is purified because it contains the love of God, and the body is improved because it holds the soul. In a passage describing the effect of the soul upon the body, Mechthild equated the soul within the body to gold within crystal:

Die sele ist in dem lichamen gebildet menschen glich,
Und hat den gôtlichen schin in ir

Und schinet dur den lichamen
Als das lúhtende golt dur die clare cristallen.

(p. 220)

The soul in the body is formed like a human being
And has the divine glow inside it
And shines through the body
As glittering gold through clear crystal.

Physical beauty results from the soul's beauty shining through the body. Thus a love for physical beauty would be a misplaced love. Eternal, genuine beauty exists in the soul alone. Physical beauty is transient and illusory, because it can not exist after the separation of the soul and the body at death.

Defined in terms of the image employed by Mechthild, the body becomes a positive substance only by the loss of its own attributes or specifically of its own flesh. Earth or solid substances are characteristically opaque. It is only the loss of opacity (the physical attributes of the flesh) that transforms the body, as sand is transformed into transparent crystal. Only the suppression of the body's physical nature by the soul can render the body acceptable to God.

The potential of the human body for eventual resurrection or acceptance into heaven indicates a possibility of a miraculous transformation of any earthly thing into a purified substance acceptable to God. Such a transformation is, however, miraculous; the essence of the miracle is the alteration of the earth substance into something of a higher nature. The nature of earthly things is impurity, and thus the natural attributes of the earth substance must be eliminated. Therefore there is found in *Das fliessende Licht* a number of solid or earth substances that, through being acted upon by a higher essence, transcend their own natural limitations. These are sanctified solids, solid substances that have lost the natural taint of earth.

The Soul as a Container for Divine Love

The potential of the body for resurrection is one example; the body is refined by the loving soul. The soul itself, however, also at times seems to be basically an earth essence. As seen in the image of the gold in crystal, the soul, like the body, is of the earth. Since gold is more precious than crystal, so is the soul more precious than the body; gold is the most precious of all metals and substances but is nevertheless of the earth. This representation of the soul is emphasized also by frequent references to the soul as a dog or a bird, the dog image [5] being a negative one demonstrating the lowliness of the soul and the bird image [6] being a positive one demonstrating the ability of the soul to fly free of the earth when in contact with God. Another image showing the soul as a solid object is the recurring one of the soul as a container ("vas") for the love of God. Just as the body is filled and improved by the loving soul, so, too, can the soul be filled and improved by the love of God. The soul without God is totally tied to the earth and, like the body without a soul dedicated to God, contains no beauty of its own; the beauty of the soul comes from God:

> Ich wart versmehet sere, do sprach vnser herre: la dich nit sere wundern; sit dc here drisem vas so verworfen und angespiet wart, was sol deñe dem essig vas geschehen, da nút gûtes iñe von im selber ist? (p. 16)

> I was greatly despised; then our Lord spoke: Do not be surprised; since the holy threefold keg was cast down and spat upon, what should then happen to the vinegar keg in which there is nothing good of itself?

This image of the soul as a container occurs several times in Mechthild's work. In the sixth book she described the flowing Trinity as filling the loving souls: "Er vlússet noch fúrbas / Und erfúllet alle diemútigen miñenvas" ("He flows still further / And fills every humble love keg") (p. 213). The most interesting use of this particular image is found in a long passage in which Mechthild confronted the question of the love relationship of God and the soul. God's capacity for love is infinite; that of the soul is limited; how then can the soul satiate God's desire for love? Mechthild resolved the question by comparing God and the soul to large and small kegs. The large keg can fill the small keg many times over; the small keg, however, must empty itself repeatedly and frequently in order to fill the larger one:

> Du bist gros und wir sint clein, wie sollen wir dir gleich werden? Herre, du hast vns gegeben und wir sóllen óch vúrbas geben. Alleine wir ein cleines vesselin sin, so hastu es doch gefúllet. Man mag ein clein vol vas so dike giessen in ein grosses vas, dc das grose vas vol wirt von dem cleinen vasse. (pp. 268–69)

> You are great and we are small; how shall we become like You? Lord, You have given to us, and we shall also give in return. Though we are a small vessel, yet You have filled it. A small, full keg can be emptied into a great keg so often that the great keg is filled by the small keg.

Only the soul that possesses love for God, however, is capable of being filled with love from God. In her description of the tormenting in purgatory of priests who had forgotten their duty to God, Mechthild portrayed the priests as broken kegs: "Si sint alle zerbrochenú vas gewesen und hant in ertrich geistliches lebeñes vergessen" ("They were all broken kegs and on earth forgot spiritual life") (p. 77). From this image it is obvious that Mechthild believed the ultimate purpose of the soul was dedication to God—the purpose of a keg is to be filled. Men who forget God have as little reason for existence as do broken kegs.

Paradoxical Earth Images of the Divine

There are many other less explicit images in *Das fliessende Licht* that represent a solid substance ennobled by the liquid it contains. In this regard may be mentioned the seemingly excessive attention that is paid to the breasts of the Virgin Mary (the source of the milk that nourished Christ) or the wounds of Christ (from which flowed the redeeming blood of the Savior). Similarly Christ himself is described as the chalice from which God's love is poured:

> der himelsche vatter da ist der seligen schenke und Jesus der kopf, der helig geist der luter win, und . . . die ganze drivaltekeit ist der volle kopf, und miñe der gewaltige keller, . . . (p. 46)

> there the heavenly Father is the blessed taverner and Jesus the chalice, the Holy Spirit the pure wine, and . . . the whole Trinity is the full chalice and love the mighty cellar, . . .

The representation of Christ as a chalice or of God as a keg would of course seem to be a contradiction of the general tendency in Mechthild's work to identify only things of the earth by means of earth imagery. But it is also true that Mechthild was less concerned with theoretical consistency than with the attractiveness of an image. Basically, however, the use of earth images to describe the Trinity appears to have arisen from an awareness of the significance of the miracle of Christ. That God should assume a human body and flesh was the supreme evidence of God's love for man. Therefore, despite the normal association of the flesh and of solids with impurity, if these things were associated with God, they were themselves purified. Thus the traditional mystic image of God is found as a mountain ("O du breñender berg" ["O You burning mountain"] [p. 8]) or, more strikingly, of God as a lodestone that draws the soul to itself upon the death of the body: "Do sprach vnser herre: Alse dc sol geschehen, so wil ich minen aten ziehen, das du mir volgest als ein agestein" ("Then spoke our Lord: Thus shall it happen that I will draw in My breath so that you will follow Me like a lodestone") (pp. 164–65).

Paradoxical descriptions of the Trinity in terms of the earth element are epitomized in Mechthild's representations of Christ. Christ miraculously assumed human flesh; thus each specific image of Christ as a lamb or a stone or fruit carries with it not only a specific significance in context but also a deeper general significance. Each image is a small reiteration of the miracle that is Christ. Each image is of earth but possesses attributes not granted to normal, impure earth substances. The metaphor of Christ as a lamb is of course a traditional image that Mechthild employed frequently but not inventively. More significant is the representation of Christ as a great rock or stone riddled with holes in which only doves and nightingales (the loving souls) may build their nests: "O du hoher stein, du bist so wol durgraben, in dir mag nieman nisten deñe tuben vnd nahtegal" ("O You lofty rock, You are so well cleft though, in You none may nest but doves and nightingales") (p. 9). Similarly in a long emblematic or allegorical vision of the Church, Mechthild described Christ as the rock upon which the Church is built:

Ich sach mit waren ŏgen miner ewekeit, in sŭsser wuñe
sunder arbeit, einen stein, der wc gelich einem gefŭgen
berge und was von im selber gewahsen, . . . Do vragete
ich den vil sŭssen stein, wer er were. Do sprach er alsust:
Ego sum Jesus. . . . Do sach ich, dc vswendig ime wc
besclossen alle vinsternisse und inwendig was er erfúllet
mit dem ewigen liehte. (p. 96)

I saw with the true eyes of my eternity, in sweet effortless
bliss, a stone that was solid as a mountain and that had
grown out of itself, ... Then I asked the sweet stone
who it was. It spoke thus : *Ego sum Jesus.* . . . Then I saw
that externally all darkness was shut off from it and internally it was filled with the everlasting light.

On this rock stands Mary, her feet adorned with jasper, a
gem representing Christian faith, which Mechthild imbued
with attributes bearing a striking resemblance to those of
the Grail in Wolfram's *Parzival*:

Der stein hat so grosses kraft, dc er vertribet die bŏsen
gitekeit von den fŭsse ir gerunge. Er git ŏch reinen smak
und reisset den heiligen hunger. Er verwiset alle vinsternisse von den ŏgen. Diser edelstein dc ist cristan gelŏbe.
(p. 96)

The stone has such great power that it drives greed from
the basis of its desire. It also gives pure taste and arouses
holy hunger. It erases all darkness from the eyes. This
precious stone is Christian belief.

The representation of Christ that seems best suited to
portray Mechthild's beliefs, however, is that of Christ as an
apple or fruit, an earth image employed in other contexts as
a symbol of evil. In a description of the Fall of Adam and
Eve, Mechthild used the traditional symbol of the apple
from the Tree of Knowledge to represent sin :

Disen bŏn han ich gesehen; er ist nit gros und sin fruht
ist vswendig vil schŏne und lustlich als ein rose, aber
inwendig ist si von nature vil sur. Dc bezeichenet den
bitteren schaden der súnden, den got nie menschen gonde.
(p. 125)

I saw this tree; it is not large and its fruit is outwardly
very beautiful and delightful as a rose, but inwardly it is
by nature very sour. That signifies the bitter harm of sins
that God never granted to man.

In spite of the significance of "fruht" as the supreme symbol
of man's sinfulness, it is also used as a symbol of Christ and,
more generally, of the gifts of God to the soul. Christ is
repeatedly presented as the fruit of the union of the dew
of the godhead and the flower that is Mary: "O nútze fruht
der schŏnen blumen!" ("O useful fruit of the beautiful
flower!") (p. 233). Fruit is the union of solid and liquid or of
earth and water as Christ is the union of man and God. An
exact parallel, with exactly opposite significance, to the Eden
apple is given in one passage in which the Trinity is a tree
and Christ is the apple: "Und da neigen ich dir den hohsten
bŏn miner heligen drivaltekeit, / So brichest du dene die
grŭnen, wissen, roten, ŏpfel miner sanftigen menscheit, . . ."
("And then I bend down to you the highest branch of My
holy Trinity, / Thus you pluck the green, white, red apples
of My gentle humanity, . . .") (p. 51). Similarly, because
Christ is the symbol of God's love for man, so is by extension
"fruht" a symbol of God's gifts to man. Christ was in effect a
gift of God the Father to man; thus Christ says: "Lieber
vatter, min nature sol ŏch fruht bringen" ("Dear Father, My
nature shall also bear fruit") (p. 69).

The gifts of God also cause the bearing of fruit within
the soul of man:

Min sunderliche gabe bringet sunderlichen wirdekeit dem
menschen an sele und an libe. Si git lere den tumben und
trost den wisen. Si git öch ewig lob und endelos ere dem
grundelosen bruñen, da si vsgevlossen ist, sweñe si mit
voller fruht wider vfswinget, da si nidervlos von mir. (pp.
187–88)

My special gift brings special worth to humanity, in soul
and in body. It gives instruction to the simple and comfort
to the wise. It also gives eternal praise and endless honor
to the bottomless spring from which it flowed, whenever
full of fruit it flows back up again to where it flowed down
from Me.

In another passage fruit becomes a simile for the good
works of man himself:

> Der gûte wille, den der gûte mensche hat
> Und in nit mag bringen ze gûter getat,
> Der glichet sich den edelen schönen blûmen
> Mit sûssem gesmake ane fruht.
>
> (p. 196)

> The good will that the good person has
> But can not change into good deeds
> Is like the noble and beautiful flowers
> With sweet smell but without fruit.

Whether Mechthild was herself consciously aware of the
dual significance of the fruit imagery in her work is question-
able; and the use of "fruht" as a metaphor both for man's
original sin and also for Christ, the ultimate salvation from
original sin, lends itself to a variety of interpretations. Perhaps the fruit is representative of all the potential fulfill-
ments for man's hunger or drive for physical and spiritual
satisfaction. Man's free will alone can decide which type of
fruit will be chosen.

Closely related to the specific image of Christ as fruit and to the concept of sanctified earth images in general is the symbol of the Virgin Mary as a flower; as Mary represents utter purity and chastity, so does the flower. Unlike the fruit that signifies the union of water and earth, the flower is entirely of the earth and is a symbol of the earth's finest manifestation. Both Mary and the flower are born of the earth but remain untainted and uncorrupted by the earth. Because Mary, according to Catholic thought, conceived without original sin, so is the flower representative of perfect earthly existence. By extension, since Mary is the ideal prototype of the mystical loving soul, so does the flower represent that which the soul strives to become.

The Wounds of Christ and the Wounding of the Soul by Love

The most important of all the sanctified solids within *Das fliessende Licht* are the body and the wounds of Christ. Because of Christ's miraculous transcendence of the flesh and the evils and limitations of earthly existence, the soul's salvation lies in a belief in, emulation of, and love for Christ. Because Christ demonstrated for man the means of subjugating the flesh, the loving soul looks to Christ for an example. And because the body and wounds of Christ demonstrate the physical counterpart to the spiritual truths that he made manifest, his body and wounds are venerated by the loving soul as tangible symbols of intangible spiritual reality. At one point Mechthild wrote, "Das allerheiligoste dc in der messe ist, dc ist gotz lichame" ("The holiest of holies in the Mass, that is God's body") (p. 210). The flsh of God, unlike the flesh of man, is incorruptible.

Perhaps because of Christ's exemplary subjugation of the flesh, Mechthild and indeed many other mystic writers were fascinated by the role of the body in the relationship of God and the soul. Because Christ was a union of spirit and flesh, he can not be adored by man on an entirely spiritual level. The body as well as the soul must be dedicated to Christ. Since the loving soul is dedicated to Christ but the body is not, the body must be made subject to the will of the soul. As a result of this dual concern with spirit and flesh in worshipping Christ, there arose an identification of certain aspects of spiritual existence with physical counterparts. Thus, there are frequent references in *Das fliessende Licht* to the concept of wounding and suffering. These are physical terms applied to a spiritual state but also ultimately, in Mechthild's case, including a secondary physical meaning. Therefore, when Mechthild has God say in a justification for his creation of man:

> Ich wil mir selben machen ein brût, dú sol mich mit iren munde grûssen und mit irem ansehen verwunden, deñe erste gat es an ein miñen. (p. 69)

> I will make for Myself a bride who shall greet Me with her mouth and wound Me with her glance, for only then does love begin.

the statement is a poetic paraphrase of the spiritual effect of love on God. Nevertheless, there is also a secondary physical implication because Christ's birth resulted from God's love for man and Christ was made to suffer the physical agony of the Crucifixion. Conversely, because of the total reciprocity of the love relationship between God and the loving soul, the soul is spiritually "wounded" by the love of God but is also expected to endure physical suffering for the sake of God. And so, when Mechthild spoke of the effect of divine love upon the soul, her intention was not only a spiritual but also a physical wounding:

Swelch mensche wird ze einer stunt
Von warer mine reht wunt,
Der wirt niemerme gesunt,
Er enkússe no denselben munt.
Von dem sin sel ist worden wunt.

(p. 37)

Whoever shall at any time
Be truly wounded by true love,
He will never again be sound
Unless he kiss the same mouth
By which his soul was wounded.

The total implication of such a passage is made abundantly
clear both by the total context of *Das fliessende Licht* and
also by such specific statements as that which appears in a
dialogue between the loving soul and the personification of
love: "Frowe miñe, ir hant verzert min fleisch und min
blût" ("Lady Love, you have devoured my flesh and blood")
(p. 4).

The wounding of Christ and the soul through love is not
merely the superficial poetic conceit that it so frequently is
in the poetry of, for example, many German Baroque poets.
Christ and the soul are wounded not by a playful Cupid but
rather by the overwhelmingly powerful figure of Love herself. Love's woundings are inflicted not by a whimsically
dainty arrow but rather by the Roman spear and the nails
that pierced the body of Christ. Physical wounds are a sign
of holiness, and physical suffering is the soul's access to God.
Martyrdom and asceticism are the hallmarks of a truly loving
soul. Mechthild wrote in a description of her vision of a
Sister Hiltegunt:

Das wisete got eim lamen hunde, der noch mit jamer
lekket sine wunden. . . . Do sprach Hiltegunt: Ich was ein
martereriñe in der fúrinen miñe, also dc dikke min herze
blût vber min hóbet gos. (p. 41)

This God showed to a lame dog that miserably is still licking its wounds. . . . Then spoke Hiltegunt: I was a martyr of fiery love so that often my heartblood poured over my head.

Christ demonstrated the ideal for mankind by his resurrection after physical suffering and death, exemplifying the transcendence of the spiritual over the physical. Physical wounds represent for Mechthild, therefore, man's potential for transcendence over his earthly environment and physical limitations. The enduring of physical suffering signifies the superiority of the soul over the body, and the emblem of physical suffering, the wounding of the flesh, becomes an object of adoration: "O blůtigů not, / O wunden tief, o smerze gros! / La mich herre nit verderben / In aller miner pinen not. Amen" ("O bloody affliction, / O deep wounds, o great pain! / Do not let me perish, Lord, / In all my suffering. Amen") (p. 234).

Mechthild's emphasis on the importance of the subjugation of the flesh is a manifestation of the more general concept of the *imitatio Christi*. Christ is the salvation of mankind because of his self-sacrifice through love; he is also the ideal of earthly existence that the loving soul must attempt to emulate. As God and man are bound to one another by love, so each sacrifices himself for the other because of love. As Christ suffered for man, so must man suffer for Christ and God. Thus, merely spiritual suffering is insufficient repayment to God. When Mechthild wrote that the soul was "gewundot mit der miñe" ("wounded by love") (p. 15), she intended physical and spiritual wounding. As Christ was resurrected after the Crucifixion, so may the soul be redeemed by an imitation of Christ's Passion; chapter 10 of book three is titled: "Von dem passio der miñenden sele die

sî von gotte hat, wie si vfstât und in den hiṁel vart" ("Of
the Passion of the loving soul that she has from God, how
she is resurrected and goes to heaven"). Then follows a
listing of the sufferings of the soul as emulation of Christ's
Passion:

> In warer liebi wirt die miñende sele verraten, in der
> súfzunge na got. . . . Si wirt an dem crúze so vaste genegelt
> mit dem haṁer der starken miñe lŏffe, dc si alle creaturen
> nit mŏgent wider gerŭffen. Si dúrstet ŏch vil sere an dem
> crúze der miñe, wan si trunke vil gerne den luteren win
> von allen gotzkinden.

> So koment si al mit alle
> Und schenkent ir die galle.
> Ir licham wirt getŏdet
> In der lebendigen miñe, . . .

(pp. 71–72)

In true love is the loving soul betrayed, in sighing after
God. . . . She is nailed to the cross by the hammer of
mighty love so firmly that all creation can not call her
down again. She also thirsts greatly on the cross of love
for she would like to drink the pure wine from all God's
children.

> Thus they come all together
> And offer gall to her.
> Her body is killed
> In living love, . . .

The essence of the *imitatio Christi* is a wounding of the
soul by Christ himself, and it is a wounding for which earth
can supply no remedy. The wounds of the soul can be
healed only if Christ lays himself in the wounds as a healing
salve:

Die wunden die er mir selber gesclagen,
Die mag ich nit langer vngesalbet tragen
Und ungebunden.
Er hat mich gewunden
Untz in den tot;
Lat er mich nu ungesalbet ligen,
So mag ich niemer genesen.

Er mûs sich selber in miner sele wunden legen.
(p. 272)

The wounds that He gave me Himself
I can no longer bear unanointed
And unbound.
He has wounded me
Nearly to death;
If He lets me lie unanointed,
Then I can never recover.

He must lay Himself in the wounds of my soul.

In these two passages Mechthild spoke only of the wounds
of the soul; but such total involvement with the soul and
its suffering implies an almost complete subjugation of the
body. The mystic could arrive at a contemplation of the
suffering of the soul through a negation of the demands of
the body. The dominance of the soul brings with it, of
necessity, a subjugation of the body. Moreover, in the passage above, "Er hat mich gewunden untz in den tot" ("He
has wounded me nearly to death") signifies the death of the
body. The key to spiritual life is physical death, just as
Christ could not be resurrected until his body had under-
gone the Crucifixion. In another passage one finds: "ich wil
und mûs vsser demselben napfe trinken, da min vater vs
getrunken hat, sol ich sin rich besitzen" ("I will and must

drink from the same goblet from which my Father drank, if I am to possess His realm") (p. 266). The suffering of Christ included physical suffering, and the suffering of the soul in imitation of Christ must also include it. Therefore, although Mechthild personally seemed to have been more acquainted with spiritual pain, she also felt the necessity of physical pain as a path to God:

> In der naht sprach ich alsus ze vnserem herren: Herre, ich wone in eime lande dc heisset ellende, dc ist disú welt, ... Daiñe han ich ein hus, dc heisset pinenvol, dc ist das hûs, da min sele iñe gevangen lit, min lichame. (p. 261

> In the night I spoke thus to our Lord: Lord, I live in a land whose name is exile, that is this world, . . . There I have a house whose name is suffering, that is the house where my soul lies imprisoned, my body.

The loving soul must emulate Christ's suffering, both spiritually and physically; and God gives both types of suffering to men "wan er wil si sinem lieben sune gelichen, der an libe und an sele gepinget wart" ("for He wants them to be like His beloved Son who was tortured in body and in soul") (p. 14).

Bernard of Clairvaux and the Sustenance of the Body

Although Mechthild obviously believed in the necessity of the subjugation and deprivation of the body as a source of spiritual strength, it is not easily determined to what lengths these beliefs extended. While it is clear that she thought the body must not be in any way pampered, it is unlikely that she believed in such eccentric excesses as self-flagellation. Any sufferings Mechthild had physically were probably the natural results of sickness and aging.

At various times she wrote of having been ill and in the passage quoted above in which she described her body as a house, "dc heisset pinenvol" ("whose name is suffering"), she was very probably speaking of the pains of old age, since the passage occurs very near the end of her work. Moreover, Mechthild lived at a Dominican convent and the Dominicans were not noted for total denial of the needs of the body. Asceticism is good for the soul, "Dis spricht vnser herre: Man sol des kúnges spise [the existence of the soul in heaven] nit vergeben hin setzen, ê man die irdenischú notdurft wol habe gessen" ("Our Lord says this: The food of the king should not be set forth in vain until earthly necessity has been eaten") (p. 187). Physical hunger and thirst bring spiritual nourishment, but physical abstinence must have limits. The theoretical basis for this attitude is found in the writings of Bernard of Clairvaux. According to Bernard, the love of God must forbear a limited love of the body. The love of God is man's duty by right; the love of the body his duty by necessity. God alone may end the physical existence of man, so man must minimally sustain his body in order to love God on earth:

> The true name for this love of the body is *necessity*. And so, in Saint Bernard's thought, there is very certainly a question of a purely natural necessity, compelling us, before everything else, to serve the needs of the body. Carnal love, taken in this sense, is opposed to the love of God only as an infirmity inherent in the animal nature, especially when fallen; man may suffer from it, he may hope to be delivered from it in another life, but it is a congenital weakness not to be overcome in this life, and for which he cannot hold himself responsible.[7]

This, too, seems to have been Mechthild's attitude toward bodily needs: the body must be fed, but only according to

60   MYSTICAL TRANSFORMATIONS

necessity. In a vision of paradise, Mechthild spoke with Enoch and Elias:

> Ich vragete în, was si lebten na menschlichen nature? Do sprach er: Wir essen ein wenig von den ôppfeln und trinken ein wenig des wassers, dc der lichame sine leblicheit behalte, und dc grôsseste ist die gotzkraft. (p. 270)

> I asked him how they lived in keeping with their human nature. Then he spoke: We eat a bit of the apples and drink a bit of the water so that the body stays alive, and the greatest thing is the power of God.

Similarly, in a much earlier passage, a dialogue between Love and the Loving Soul, Mechthild made an equivalent statement but with a dual meaning:

> So man die gevangenen nút wil haben tot,
> So git man inen wasser und brot.
> Die artzenie, die dir got dikke hat gegeben,
> Das ist anders nút deñe ein vristunge in dis mônschliche leben.
>
> (p. 6)

> So that the prisoners will not die
> They are given water and bread.
> The medicine that God has often given you
> Is nothing more than a respite in this mortal life.

Here the "gevangenen" ("prisoners") are the souls of men trapped not only within the love of God but also within the body. Because the body must be sustained by the minimum of food, so must God sustain the soul by granting it as much of divine gifts and love as he deems necessary. That is to say, the soul's experience of God on earth is like the food of a prisoner when compared to the experience of God once the soul reaches heaven.

For obvious reasons Mechthild's comments on orthodox Catholic dietary restrictions correspond to her general deprecation of the flesh as an earth substance. She praised monks who eat sparingly and avoid meat completely: "Si . . .sônt bi den gemeinen lúten essen und trinken alle die spise die si inen gebent, ane vleisch alleine" ("They shall eat and drink with the common people any food they are given, with the exception of meat") (p. 122). The flesh of animals is impure and identified with the flesh of man; thus, the eating of meat becomes a symbol of physical indulgence that must be avoided:

Heliger lúte leben dc sint alles fritage, wan si vastent alles von súnden, und si essent nit die verbotten spise, mere si lebent nach gótlicher wise. (p. 114)

The lives of holy people are nothing but Fridays, for they fast in everything due to sins, and they do not eat the forbidden food, rather they live as divinely instructed.

This adherence to dietary restrictions is merely one more specific manifestation of the general deprecation of the body and of all earth substances in Mechthild's work. In spite of certain exceptions, as discussed above, earth images in *Das fliessende Licht* are generally negative, representing corruption, sin, transience, and evil. They represent the earthly existence of man, an existence that can be transcended only through the grace and love of God for man. In terms of the elemental image groups within *Das fliessende Licht,* earth images symbolize a physical existence that can be transcended only by contact with a higher elemental realm, most usually that of water, the transitional element.

Two examples of this type of imagery in Mechthild's work indicate the nature of man's existence. In one passage the life of man on earth is described as a desert:

Du solt miñen das niht,
Du solt vliehen das iht,

Du solt das wasser der pine trinken
Und das fúr der miñe mit dem holtz der tugende entzúnden,
So wonest du in der waren wústenunge.

(p. 17)

You should love the nothing,
You should flee the something,

You should drink the water of pain
And light the fire of love with the wood of virtue,
Thus will you live in the true desert.

By contrasting the words *niht* and *iht*, Mechthild epitomized
the duality of man's existence. Man must love the "niht"
(God or the spirituality of man) and must flee the "iht" (the
material, the physical, the flesh of existence). The "wasser"
of suffering and "fúr" of love provide man's sustenance on
earth. Similarly in a later passage, man's existence is represented as a barren field on which nothing good will grow
until it receives the water and the fire of the Trinity:

Herre, min irdensch wesen stat vor minen ŏgen,
Gelich einem dúrren akker,
Da wenig gûtes uffe ist gewahsen.
Eya sûsser Jesu Christe,
Nu sende mir den sûssen regen diner menscheit
Und die heisse suñen diner lebendigen gotheit
Und den milten towe des heiligen geistes,
Dc ich verclage min herzeleit.

(p. 100)

Lord, my earthly being stands before my eyes
Like a barren field
Where little good has grown.

Oh sweet Jesus Christ,
Now send me the sweet rain of Your humanity,
And the hot sun of Your living divinity,
And the gentle dew of the Holy Spirit
So that I may plead the sorrow of my heart.

In this way Mechthild associated all the things of the earth and man's earthly existence with sterility, at best, and damnation, at worst. Only through contact with the higher elemental realms—water, air, and fire—can the substances and limitations of earth be transformed or transcended.

Notes to Chapter 2

1. Arthur O. Lovejoy, *The Great Chain of Being, A Study of the History of an Idea* (Cambridge, Mass.: Harvard University Press, 1966), p. 59.
2. Ibid., p. 89.
3. Aristotle, cited by Sambursky, p. 91.
4. Thomas Aquinas, cited by Lovejoy, p. 79.
5. Pp. 30, 41, 50, 66, 90, and 278, for example.
6. Pp. 5, 10, 17, 27, 37, 163, 240, 273, and 280.
7. Etienne Gilson, *The Mystical Theology of Saint Bernard,* trans. A. H. C. Downes (London and New York: Sheed and Ward, 1940), p. 40.

3

The Origins of Mechthild's
Water Symbolism

In *Das fliessende Licht* both the loving interaction of God
and man and the mystical transition of the soul to God are
consistently represented by the imagery of liquids. Mechthild's God approaches man within the realm of water and
the loving soul of man responds to God by shedding its
earthly attributes and assuming liquid or fluid characteristics. Pursuing the love of God, the soul, like gold or wax in
fire, liquefies and begins to flow toward and with God. Ap-
proached by the flood of God's love, the soul imitates God,
becoming fluid: "So zůchet er si, so vlúset si" ("when He
draws her, then she flows") (p. 7) or "so begiñet er minenk-
lich ze lúhtende gegen der sele und si begiñet ze vliessende
von herzklicher liebi" ("thus He begins to shine lovingly on
the soul and she begins to flow from heartfelt love") (p. 176).
Ultimately the soul becomes, like God himself, a spring or
brook: "Du bist . . . ein bach miner hitze" ("You are . . . a
brook for My heat") (p. 10).

There are several causes for the predominance of the
imagery of water and liquids in Mechthild's work: the

tangibility of water; the transitional position of the sphere of water within the cosmos; the practical significance of water as a purifying agent; the traditional symbolism of liquids in the Bible and in the sacraments of the Church; and perhaps even the archetypal or psychological symbolism of water in the hypothetical collective unconscious of mankind. A combination of all these influences best accounts for Mechthild's reliance on this central imagery.

The tangibility of water and its transitional significance have already been discussed. Water's practical significance is immediately obvious. Leaving aside all abstract implications, water is the most common, most expedient means of cleansing that which is soiled. Moreover, applying this practical concept to the elemental system found in Mechthild's work and to its symbolic significance, one sees that water would be the most obvious means to remove from the soul the earthly taint caused by the soul's imprisonment in the body.

The common sense significance of water, however, would not entirely explain the profusion of liquid images in Mechthild's work. *Das fliessende Licht* was strongly influenced by tradition, both in subject matter and imagery. Mechthild's significance as a poet lies not in originality of thought but rather in originality of treatment. As any nun or Beguine of her era would have been, Mechthild was extremely familiar with at least the more superficial and popular aspects of the Christian tradition. Thus, it is only to be expected that the imagery of the Old and New Testaments should have found its way into her work.

Biblical Water Symbolism

It has been noted that because Judaism and Christianity originated in an area where water is scarce, it is only natural that water should have assumed a great significance for the authors of the Bible and that god or the works of God should so often have been represented by the giving and taking away of water. Whether or not this is the primary reason, it is nevertheless undeniable that water in one form or another has a central significance for many stories in the Bible.[1] To give only the most obvious examples, water plays an important role in Genesis, Exodus, the Psalms, and the Prophets in the Old Testament and in the Gospels of the New Testament.

It is significant, however, that Mechthild's water imagery is derived principally from the New Testament; water imagery in the Old Testament is used primarily to depict an aspect of God with which Mechthild was little concerned. In the Psalms is described the division of the ocean; in Exodus is found the parting of the waters of the Red Sea to let pass Israel but to destroy Pharaoh; and the story of Noah's Ark in Genesis relates the flooding of the earth by God and the physical and spiritual destruction of most of mankind. These examples demonstrate an aspect of water symbolism that, for the most part, is lacking in *Das fliessende Licht;* these stories represent water as a manifestation of a deity of creation and retribution. Although Mechthild does at times refer to one or another of these stories, as when she speaks of the drowning of Pharaoh: "Und pharao und sin frúnde, / Die sǒnt vns nit volgen alze verre. / O we, wie sint si ertrunken in disem mere!" ("And Pharaoh and his friends, / They should not follow us too far. / Alas, how they are drowned in this sea") (p. 81), she nevertheless is less concerned with the wrathful, retributive God of the Old Testament than she is with the loving, merciful God of the Christian era.

As can be seen from her reference to the Red Sea story, Mechthild is aware of water's destructive potential, but she chose to ignore this aspect of God as water in favor of gentler divine representations. Mechthild's ultimate concern was union with a loving, personal God, and He manifests Himself therefore as a stream, a spring, dew, or rain: nondestructive representations of God's love for man. There is also abundant justification for this type of representation to be found in the Bible, even in the Old Testament. One can find numerous references to the fertility and regenerative properties of water when it falls upon dry ground. Jeremiah represents God as a fountain of living waters (Jeremiah 2:13). Ezekiel speaks of the waters that flow out from under the temple (Ezekiel 47). Certainly more significant, however, are the frequent associations of water with the life and deeds of Christ in the New Testament, particularly in the Gospel of John: the transforming of water into wine at the marriage feast at Cana (John 2:3–10); the effecting of miraculous cures by means of pools of water at Bethsaide (John 5:4) and Siloe (John 9:6); the washing of the feet of the Apostles (John 13:5); Christ's walking upon the water (John 6:19); and the flowing of water and blood from Christ's side during the Crucifixion (John 19:34). Moreover, in chapters 3, 4, and 7 of the Gospel of John, Christ uses water images to describe the spiritual rebirth and eternal life that He offers man:

> Jesus answered, "Amen, amen, I say to thee, unless a man be born again of water and the Spirit, he cannot enter into the kingdom of God." (John 3:5)

> Jesus answered . . . , "If thou didst know the gift of God, and who it is who says to thee, 'Give me to drink,' thou, perhaps, wouldst have asked of him, and he would have given thee living water. . . . He, however, who drinks of the water that I will give him shall never thirst; but the water that I will give him shall become in him

a fountain of water, springing up into life everlasting." (John 4:10–14)

"If anyone thirst, let him come to me and drink. He who believes in me, as the Scripture says, *From within him there shall flow rivers of living water.*" (John 7:37–38)

And finally must be mentioned the waters of Christ's baptism in the Jordan by John the Baptist.

Baptismal Water and Sacramental Liquids

Precisely this association of water with Christ is reflected in the use of water in many of the sacraments of the medieval Church; and it is this association with which Mechthild was most concerned. In the rites of the Church, water was and is still a central element. Water is used in the rite of confirmation to membership in the Church. Water is placed at the entrance to churches as a part of an entrance ritual, and the peculiar significance that such a ritual could assume for a mystically inclined believer is demonstrated by a story about Saint Theresa of Avila who is said to have put perfume into the holy water so that she would be attractive to her divine lover.

More important than these uses of water, however, is the significance of water in the rite of baptism. Through the influence of Saint Paul, who is probably most responsible for the growth of mysticism within the Church, baptism assumed central significance for the spiritual life of any Christian. Citing various Biblical passages as evidence, Rudolf Schnackenburg has attempted to demonstrate all the various meanings that Saint Paul ascribed to the baptism ritual. Baptism represents, spiritually, a bath of cleansing and of regeneration first of all, second, an assignment to

Christ and an incorporation in Christ, third, a "Salvation-Event," and finally, a sacramental dying and rising again with Christ (indirectly implying both the *imitatio Christi* and the *unio mystica*).[2]

Similarly Albert Schweitzer in *The Mysticism of Paul the Apostle* demonstrated the development of the rite of baptism from the Prophets of the Old Testament to John the Baptist to Paul. Tracing the origins and history of Christian baptism, Schweitzer perceived its beginnings in the Old Testament books of Ezekiel, Isaiah, Zachariah, and Jeremiah, which prescribe purification with water as a preparation for the final judgment of man by God. For John the Baptist, baptism became not only a preparation for man's final judgment but also a guarantee of the effectiveness of repentance. Significantly, Schweitzer distinguished between the baptism of Christ and the baptisms of the followers of Christ, a distinction also found in Mechthild's work. Quoting Ignatius, Schweitzer wrote that the followers of Christ are purified by the water of baptism but that Christ himself "was born and baptized in order that by His passion He might purify the water." [3] It is, however, the Pauline concept of baptism that is probably most important for the study of water and baptism in *Das fliessende Licht:*

> The forgiveness of sins is for Paul effected in baptism because, through the dying and rising again which takes place in it, *the fleshly body and the sin which cleaves to it are abolished,* and henceforth are as though they were not. Along with the flesh, sin is destroyed and does not count anymore [italics added].[4]

It is this abolishment of the flesh and its attendant sin that is a primary goal of Mechthild and most Christian mystics. This idea in Paul's thought implies the total dichotomy of body and soul that predominates in medieval mystical writing. The abolishment of the flesh can be effected by baptism. Water, by its presence in baptism, becomes a substance antagonistic to flesh and sin.

Thus, water by virtue of its association with Christ and with the rituals of the Church assumed characteristics that transcend the merely physical attributes of water. Of this transcendent symbolism of water, F. W. Dillistone has written:

> it becomes apparent how in creation, in Scripture, and in the life of the Church, water is a most suggestive and expansive symbol to denote the operations of the Spirit within the organism of the Body of Christ. Water is not just a sign of cleansing; it is a symbol of new creation and fertilisation and refreshment and regeneration.[5]

In a discussion of the elemental theories that were prevalent in Western thought until nearly the eighteenth century, John Read asserts that "all liquid substances were supposed to be liquid because they possessed something in common; this hypothetical substance was called the *Element, Water*."[6] Because of this identification of all liquid substances, it seems justifiable to assume that liquids other than water, such as blood, milk, wine, and honey, are also capable of representing the transcendent and positive qualities more normally attributed to water. Beyond such medieval hypotheses of the interrelatedness of all liquids, Dillistone discerns a symbolic relationship between the waters of baptism and the blood of the Crucifixion. Attempting to demonstrate a traditional linking of water and blood, Dillistone cites a passage from Exodus in which "blood is sprinkled on the people before the covenant is consummated in the common feast."[7] According to Dillistone, there is an inherent similarity in the water and the blood of Christ symbolizing a similarity of the Baptism and the Crucifixion:

> This baptism of Christ was of a double kind; it was a baptism of initiation in the waters of the Jordan, it was a baptism of suffering on the hill of Calvary.[8]

The equation of water and blood is, of course, made even more explicit in the New Testament. According to the Gospel of John, after Christ's death his side was pierced by the lance of a Roman soldier and water and blood flowed together from the wound: "one of the soldiers opened his side with a lance, and immediately there came out blood and water" (John 19:34). John, moreover, emphasizes the symbolic significance of water and blood in his First Epistle:

> This is He who came in water and in blood, Jesus Christ; not in the water only, but in the water and the blood. . . . And there are three that bear witness on earth: the Spirit, and the water, and the blood; and these three are one. (1 John 5:6–8)

The similarity of water and blood specifically and of all liquids generally is further emphasized by the obvious symbolism of the wine used in the celebration of the Eucharist. The identification of blood and wine arises from the words of Christ at the Last Supper. Giving the wine to the Apostles, "he said to them, 'This is my blood of the new covenant, which is being shed for many'" (Mark 14:23; also Matt. 26:28; Luke 22:20; and I Cor. 11:25). Similarly oil, too, because of its use in extreme unction and other sacraments of the Church, takes on a transcendent significance; it is, according to Dillistone, a sign of God's ownership.[9]

It must be noted that these liquids—water, blood, wine, and oil—are identified with one another in Christian tradition less because of their similar physical properties than because of the similarly positive qualities attributed to them because of their employment in the sacraments. It nevertheless seems very likely that the similar symbolic meanings ascribed by the orthodox Church to these specific liquids would have, in effect, served as a reinforcement for the medieval idea of the similarity of all liquids as "water." This idea is further emphasized if one considers the medieval concept of the four humors according to which each person receives specific personal characteristics from the combination of these primary liquids—blood, black bile, yellow bile, and phlegm—within the body. The four humors, sustaining the life of the body, represent water as vitalism.

Psychological Bases for Mechthild's Water Symbolism

In addition to the importance of the physical qualities of water, Biblical references to water, and the importance of water and other liquids in the Sacraments, there should be mentioned the possible psychological bases for water symbolism in *Das fliessende Licht*. C. G. Jung discussed psychological symbolism and archetypal symbols in works such as *The Integration of the Personality* and *The Psychology of the Unconscious*. Building on the work of Jung, various writers such as Dillistone in *Christianity and Symbolism* and Joseph Campbell in *The Hero with a Thousand Faces* have attempted to demonstrate the universally recurrent and subconscious symbolism of dreams, myths, and religions. In Dillistone's discussion of basic water symbolism are found, in a synopsis of Jung's ideas, three archetypal meanings of water:

(1) Water from the heavens has been regarded as posses-
    sing life-giving properties . . .
(2) Water gushing from the earth has been regarded as
    issuing from the womb of the Earth-Mother . . .
(3) Still water, the water of darkness, has also in some
    way been associated with the womb and to be
    plunged in this water has been regarded as a means
    of gaining the gift of immortality.[10]

Although to apply such a symbolic scheme to the water
imagery in *Das fliessende Licht* is to oversimplify the symbolic significance of this imagery, nevertheless, all three of
Dillistone's archetypes do appear in Mechthild's work. Rein-
forcing a psychological interpretation of a visionary work
such as *Das fliessende Licht*, Marghanita Laski has demonstrated a similarity between the characteristics of ecstasy—
the mystical experience of visions and union with the divine
—and the characteristics of the psychological condition of
manic-depression.[11]

In spite of this linking of religious symbolism with psychology and with the symbols of mankind's collective unconscious, such psychological investigation is more applic-
able to the literary and religious traditions in which Mechthild's work stands than it is to her imagery itself. In other
words, Mechthild's image of God as a gushing spring probably bears an ultimate relationship to the second of Dillistone's archetypes, but it is unlikely that this was consciously intended by Mechthild. While archetypal interpretations
may be justifiable for the religious tradition that Mechthild
had inherited, they are further removed from her conscious
intention than are the Biblical and sacramental implications
of the water imagery in *Das fliessende Licht*.

Notes to Chapter 3

1. The frequency of references to water and all its various forms is affirmed by reference to a Bible concordance. Robert Young (*Analytical Concordance to the Bible*, 22d American edition, revised by William B. Stevenson [New York: Funk & Wagnalls Company, 1955]) lists, for example, 392 references for the word *sea;* 240 for *river;* 53 for *thirst;* 56 for *spring;* 39 for *fountain;* and so forth.

2. Rudolph Schnackenburg, *Baptism in the Thought of Saint Paul, A Study in Pauline Theology,* trans. G. R. Beasley-Murray (New York: Herder and Herder, 1964.)

3. Albert Schweitzer, *The Mysticism of Paul the Apostle,* trans. William Montgomery (New York: The Seabury Press, 1968), p. 234.

4. Schweitzer, pp. 262–63.

5. Frederick W. Dillistone, *Christianity and Symbolism* (Philadelphia: The Westminster Press, 1955), p. 210.

6. John Read, *Prelude to Chemistry, An Outline of Alchemy* (Cambridge, Mass.: The M.I.T. Press, 1961), p. 11.

7. Dillistone, p. 213.

8. Dillistone, p. 211. For Mechthild, both the Baptism and the Crucifixion are demonstrations of God's love for man. For Dillistone, both water and blood represent baptism and initiation; for Mechthild, they represent divine love.

9. Dillistone, p. 202.

10. Dillistone, p. 186.

11. Marghanita Laski, *Ecstasy. A Study of Some Secular and Religious Experiences* (Bloomington, Ind.: Indiana University Press, 1962).

4

Motion and Freedom as Characteristics of the Imagery of Liquids

Mechthild at times characterized the Trinity and God the Father by means of images of fire and the sun, images that, according to Lüers, are derived from traditional metaphors for the divine.[1] The Loving Soul of Mechthild's work refers to God as: "O du breñender berg, o du vserwelte suñe!" ("O You burning mountain, o You chosen sun!") (p. 8) and says later: ". . . dú gotheit ist so fúrig heiss . . ." (". . . the divinity is so fiery hot . . .") (p. 21). The representation of God by fire imagery is further explainable by the position of the sphere of fire within the cosmos. Fire is the elemental sphere that lies farthest from the earth and closest to heaven, and fire was therefore thought to be the element most similar in natural attributes to God himself.

The preponderance of Mechthild's images for the manifestations of God are images of water rather than of fire, however. The element fire is for Mechthild representative of the unbearable force or strength of God and of the erotic passion of God for the human soul. It is the manifestation of God that is beyond the power of man to endure and that would overwhelm man with its utter magnificence: "der gŏtlichen miñe vúrige kraft gaht v́ber alle menschliche maht" ("Divine love's fiery power surpasses all human might") (p. 164). In her descriptions of the birth of Christ, Mechthild implied that, of all mortals, Mary alone was able to withstand the ultimate fiery force of God and only then through God's grace:

> Und die kraft der heligen drivaltekeit hatte din nature also bedruket . . . und dú ewig wisheit der almehtigen gotheit hatte dir, frŏwe, einen schatten gegeben da du iñe behieltest din menschlich leben . . . und dc ŏch dine blŭmende menscheit in der suñen der creftigen gotheit nit verswinde. (p. 65)

> And the strength of the Holy Trinity had thus suppressed your nature . . . and the eternal wisdom of the almighty divinity had given you a shadow, Lady, so that you kept your mortal life . . . and so also that your blossoming humanity did not vanish in the sun of the mighty divinity.

God as fire is God the creator—omniscient, omnipotent, and omnipresent—and a God of devastating splendor. The manifestation of God with which Mechthild is most concerned, however, is a personal and tangible God of love and mercy. Mechthild's God is drawn to the soul of man by the power of love; and, because of his love for man, he seeks to relinquish his fiery heat:

> Do sprach vnser herre zŭ mir: gŏñe mir dis, dc ich die hitze miner gotheit, dú gerunge miner mŏnscheit und den lust des heligen geistes mit dir kŭlen mŭge. (p. 106)

> Thus spoke our Lord to me: grant Me this, that with you I might cool the heat of My divinity, the desires of My humanity, and the pleasure of the Holy Spirit.

Thus God seeks not the annihilation of man but rather a loving interaction with him, even during man's existence on earth. God as fire represents pain for the body and darkness for the soul. Thus, following the above passage in which God as fire does approach the soul, one finds: "Hienach kam dú brut in so grosser vinsternisse, dc der licham swiste vnde kramp in der pine" ("Afterwards the bride came into such great darkness that the body sweated and was cramped with pain") (p. 106). Therefore, Mechthild's merciful God predominantly manifests himself not as fire but as water, the transitional element that brings regeneration rather than suffering to the soul and that simultaneously combines purity and tangibility.

Mechthild's Loving Soul is, as might be expected, a feminine being as a counterpart to the conception of God as masculine. The Loving Soul is not totally passive as a result of its femininity, however. In the interaction of God and the soul it is, to be sure, God who initiates and then dominates. The soul, stimulated by its awareness of God, nevertheless becomes active in its search for God. The soul does not passively wait for God but rather seeks him out ("Ich bin ein vollewachsen brût, / Ich wil gan nach minem trût" ["I am a full-grown bride, / I want to go to my groom"] [p. 21]). Having found God, the soul does not merely passively accept him but rather responds actively to him. Within the love relationship, God and the soul are unequal but coactive partners. Mechthild's God needs the love and attention of the soul as much as the soul needs him. He is a God who does not overwhelm the soul and leave it senseless; he submits to the soul's embrace and permits himself to be apprehended totally by the soul. Thus, Mechthild was primarily concerned with the depiction of a tangible and apprehensible divinity:

Den nim ich, minste sele, in den arm min,
Und isse in und trinke in
Und tůn mit im was ich wil.

(p. 43)

I, the least of souls, will take Him in my arms,
And eat Him and drink Him
And do with Him what I will.

If God is to be held in the arms of the soul, he must be represented by means of imagery representing substance, if not solidity, and purity. Water, unlike earth, is untainted but is also simultaneously apprehensible by the senses of man. It can be held in one's hands even if only temporarily, just as the mystics believed that God could be temporarily held by the soul within the *unio mystica.*

"Vliessen" and Mechthild's Concept of God

One image that recurs throughout Mechthild's work and that demonstrates her concept of a personal, loving God is that of God as a flood or "vlůt," the motion of which is "vliessen." This image and variations of it occur again and again but always in respect to that aspect of the divinity that lovingly interacts with the soul. Particularly in the early books, Mechthild's almost exclusive concern is the depiction of her personalized concept of God, and here she emphasized the totality of God as a spring ("brune") from which God's love for man flows inexhaustibly. In the later books, apparently having become less introspective and more aware of her society, of the Church, and of the Church's dogma, Mechthild began to regard God as a combination of love, power, and justice rather than merely as an inexhaustible bestower of divine grace.

Mechthild's later work is less concerned with the portrayal of truly individual mystical experience and more blatantly didactic. The tone of the early work is intensely personal and conveys an individual's immediate experience of God; the later work, on the other hand, emphasizes not individual experience but rather the salvation of the souls of all men. This change in thought is reflected in a change in theme and imagery. In the later books Mechthild more frequently represented God as fire; she spoke more often of the necessity for earthly sufferings as preparation for salvation; she even attributed a destructive potential to the normally nondestructive imagery of water.

In the second chapter of book 1 one finds: "Der ware gottes grůs, der da kumet von dem himelschen flůt vs dem bruñen der vliessenden drivaltekeit" ("God's true greeting that comes from the heavenly flood out of the spring of the flowing Trinity") (p. 4), and again in the same chapter: "Dis ist ein grůs . . . , der dringet usser dem vliessenden gotte in die armen, dúrren sele . . ." ("This is a greeting . . . that rushes from the flowing God into the poor, arid soul . . .") (p. 5). God's initiation of a love relationship with the soul is thus described as a greeting that has its source in the spring that is God or the Trinity. This particular image remains relatively unchanged, as can be seen from a similar passage from book 5: "Des vaters stiñe sprichet ime lobesange: Ich bin ein vsvliessende bruñe, den nieman erschŏpfen mag" ("The Father's voice speaks in a song of praise: I am a gushing spring that no one can exhaust") (p. 158). In book 5, however, Mechthild was also aware of God's destructive potential, an awareness that is not present in the earlier books. God says to the soul:

> Min widergrůs ist ein so gros hiñelvlůt,
> Solte ich mich in dich nach miner maht geben
> Du behieltest nit dein mensclich leben.

(p. 143)

My greeting in return is a heavenly flood so great
That if I should give Myself to you with all My power
You would lose your mortal life.

In the early books God's capacity for love is accepted very
openly by the Loving Soul or by Mechthild; by the time of
the above passage, however, this receptivity has become
inhibited by an awe-filled respect or perhaps fear of the
potentially overwhelming power of God. Also in the later
books there are more frequent references to God's justice
and righteousness; in book 7 Mechthild envisioned the scale
of God's justice weighing souls on the Day of Judgment:

> Ich bin gotz gerehtekeit,
> Gotz gerihte dc wart mir gegeben, dc ist min,
> Do Adam in dem paradyso súnde tet.
> Min gerihte hat gewesen lange und gros; . . . .
>
> (p. 275)

> I am God's righteousness,
> God's judgment that was given to me, that is mine,
> Because Adam sinned in paradise.
> My judgment was long and heavy; . . .

Even though the passage goes on to say that God's justice
is tempered by mercy ("barmherzekeit"), it is still clear that
by the end of *Das fliessende Licht* God's love is no longer
given freely—as it was in the early books—but must be
earned by the soul.

Although the preoccupation with God as Love is dimin-
ished in Mechthild's later work, nevertheless, there are
found throughout her work images of God or the Trinity as
a spring and of God's grace or his love for man as the flood
that arises from the spring. These images are consistently
representative of manifestations of God as love, and Mechthild built upon this fundamental concept to create more

complex representations of the interaction of God and the Loving Soul. One example of this is found in book 1 in which Mechthild described the soul as a hunted deer that drinks from the spring that is God: "Und kunt gelöffen als ein verjageter hirze / Nach dem bruñen der ich bin" ("And comes running like a hunted deer / To the spring that is I") (p. 17).

This metaphor of God as a spring emphasizes that the product of the spring—the water—is more a symbol of God's gifts to the soul, of God's love for the soul, or of divine grace than it is a symbol of God himself. God is the source of the liquids or water that nourish the soul of man. Thus, one finds frequent references to God's love for man as a "miñevlût": "Dú clare miñe von spilender flût / Tût der sele sûsse not" (p.75), or, "Din sûssen minenden bruñenvlússe / Vertilgent alles min herzeleit" (p. 239) ("Pure love from the swirling flood / Gives the soul sweet distress," or, "Your sweet loving spring-flow / Extinguishes all my heart's pain"). This image is found again in a chapter that, curiously enough, occurs in book 6 in prose and is then repeated in book 7 in verse: "dc ist die spilende miñevlût, die von got heimlich in dú sele vlússet und si wider mit siner kraft nach îr maht" ("it is the swirling flood of love that secretly flows from God into the soul and the soul flows back with His strength to the best of her ability") (pp. 199 and 259). This combination of God, love, and water is employed more subtly in a long chapter in book 1 in which Mechthild described a metaphorical landscape of love tinged with eroticism. Christ as a beautiful youth tells the Loving Soul as a maiden to come to the shadow of the spring, to the bed of love: "kument ze mitten tage zu dem bruñen schatten in das bette der miñe, da sônt ir úch mit im erkûlen" ("come at midday to the shadow of the spring to the bed of love, there you shall cool yourself with Him") (p. 20).

"Vliessen" and Divine Creativity

As divine love is a gift of God to the soul and a sign of divine grace, so too are other divine gifts represented by Mechthild as a "vlůt" from heaven. At one point in a defense against hostile criticism, Mechthild described her revelations as a gift that flowed to her because of her lowliness. She attempted to show that, because of her own ignorance, she was a more likely recipient of God's truths than was an educated priest. Skillfully extending her liquid metaphor, she asserted that, since water naturally seeks the lowest level, so did God's truths naturally flow to her, the lowest point in humanity:

> Die hosten berge mögent nit enpfan
> Die offenbarunge miner gnaden,
> Wan die vlůt mines heligen geistes
> Vlůsset von nature ze tal.

(p. 53)

> The highest mountains may not receive
> The revelations of My grace,
> For the flood of My Holy Spirit
> By nature flows into the valleys.

Mechthild's intention in this passage is emphasized by her use of the word *vliessen* in other passages relating to the writing of her book of revelations. Her revelations flowed to her from God and she merely recorded them. This use of the word *vliessen* is apparent even in the title of Mechthild's work and is elucidated in book 1 in which her work was viewed as a flowing from God to Mechthild and past her to her fellow Christians:

> Eya herre, wie sol dis bůch heissen, alleine ze dinen eren? Es sol heissen: ein vliessende lieht miner gotheit, in allů die herzen die da lebent ane valscheit. (p. 3)

Ah, Lord, what shall this book be named, only to honor You? It shall be named: a flowing light of My divinity into all the hearts who live there without dishonesty.

Similarly in book 6, Mechthild described herself merely as God's tool:

> Dise schrift die in disem bůche stat, die ist gevlossen vs von der lebenden gotheit in Swester Mehtilden herze und ist also getrúwelich hie gesetzet, alse si vs von irme herzen gegeben ist von gotte und geschriben von iren henden. (p. 215)

The writing found in this book has flowed out from the living divinity into Sister Mechthild's heart and is faithfully set down here as it was given out by her heart from God and written by her hand.

The same thought is employed as a defense against criticism. Mechthild said that those critics who threatened to burn her book would burn not the work of a human being but rather the work and truth of God:

Ich wart von disem buche gewarnet,
Und wart von menschen also gesaget;
Wolte man es nit bewaren,
Da mǒhte ein brant úbervaren.

[God speaks to Mechthild:] lieb minú, betrůbe dich nit ze verre,
Die warheit mag nieman verbreñen.

Dc bůch ist drivaltig
Und bezeichent alleine mich.

Dú wort bezeichent mine wunderliche gotheit,
Dú vliessent von stunde ze stunde
In dine sele us minem gôtlichen munde.
Dú stime der worte bezeichent minen lebendigen geist
Und vollebringent mit ir selben die rehten warheit.

(p. 52)

I was warned about this book
And was told by people:
It ought not to be preserved
But given to the flames.

(God speaks to Mechthild) My love, do not be too con-
    cerned,
No one may burn the truth.

The book is threefold
And represents Me alone.

My miraculous divinity is represented by the words
That flow from hour to hour
Into your soul from My divine mouth.
The voice of the words represents My living spirit
And fulfills in itself the actual truth.

As "vliessen" represents creativity from God, so does it
by extension represent spiritual procreation. All that comes
from God flows from God as from a spring and "vliessen"
represents the birth and life of the soul. Interestingly contrasted to the idea of spiritual procreation ("vliessen") is the
use of the word *gebern* to describe physical procreation. The
antitheses "vliessen" and "gebern" specifically illustrate the
general antitheses, spirit and flesh. In a description of the
birth of Christ as man, Mechthild employed both words in

order to emphasize the paradox that Christ embodies and then, equating the human soul with Christ, to describe the soul:

> Herre Jesu Christe, der du bist *gevlossen* sunder begine us dem herzen dines ewigen vatters *geistlich,* und *geborn* von einer lutern ganzen maget, Sante Marien *fleische,* . . . . Herre, ewiger vatter, . . . ich, aller menschen vnwirdigeste, óch vs dinem herzen *gevlossen* bin *geistlich,* und ich, herre Jesu criste, *geboren* us diner siten *vleischlich,* und ich, herre, Got und Mensche, mit v́wer beder geist gereinget bin, . . . [italics added]. (p. 135)

> Lord Jesus Christ, Who *flowed* in the *spirit* without beginning out of the heart of Your eternal Father and were *born* from a pure and immaculate maid, Saint Mary's *flesh,* . . . Lord, eternal Father, . . . I, the most unworthy of all people, also *flowed* in the *spirit* out of Your heart, and I, Lord Jesus Christ, was *born* out of Your side as *flesh,* and I, Lord, God and Man, am purified by both Your spirits.

The Freedom of the Soul

The word *geboren* to describe the physical birth of Christ represents the assumption of physical form by that which had been completely spirit and, therefore, free from the limitations of the flesh. So conversely the word *gevlossen* to describe the spiritual birth of man represents man's potential for freedom from the ties of the flesh. Mechthild believed that the human soul during its sojourn on earth is trapped within the human body. Because of its entrapment within the body, the soul is bound to the earth and denied the freedom that it would enjoy without the physical bonds. One of the most predominant and significant characteristics of Mechthild's descriptions of the experience of the soul in heaven is that of the utter freedom that the soul enjoys.

This heavenly freedom is described by Mechthild by means of images of motion. Motion unencumbered by any restraint is her idea of freedom.

Because the essence of "vliessen" is motion, "vliessen" becomes a metaphor of freedom. That "vliessen" implies freedom is emphasized by the frequent use, in combination with "vliessen," of the words *spilen* or *spil* that demonstrate the willingness and in fact the eagerness of the soul to begin moving and the utter joy that the soul derives from its free movement. Thus the word *spil* is used as a synonym for the *unio mystica*, the temporary freedom of the soul:

> er [God] wil alleine mit ir [the soul] spilen ein spil das der lichame nút weis, noch die dörper bi dem phlûge noch die Ritter in dem turnei, ... (p. 5)

> only with her will He play a game that the body does not know nor the peasants at the plow nor the knights in the joust, . . .

Similarly in another passage Mechthild described the blissful rewards of the loving souls who take their passion to Christ:

> Wie si [the souls] deñe mit dir [Christ] spilent und dinen miñelust in sich verzerent, dc ist so himellichú sůssekeit und so notliche vereinikeit, dc ich desgliches nit weis. (p. 60)

> How they then play with You and devour Your desire for love; that is such heavenly sweetness and such urgent union that I know nothing like it.

As is implied by the words *spilen* and *vliessen*, the soul within the *unio mystica* or in contact with God loses the static quality that is the hallmark of earthly existence and begins to move, to flow, to play, and to become free. In the following description of the onset of the *unio mystica,* there is a multiplicity of action verbs that demonstrate the soul's loss of its static condition within the union:

> so begiñet er [Christ] minenklich ze lúhtende gegen der sele und si begiñet ze vliessende von herzklicher liebi. Da verlúret dú sele alle ir schulde und allen iren jamer, und so begiñet er si ze lerende allen sinen willen. So begiñet si ze smekende sine sůssekeit und so begiñet er si ze grůssende . . . und so begiñet er si ze trutende, dc si krank wirt. So begiñet si ze sugende, dc er miñesiech wirt . . . . (p. 176)

> then He begins to shine with love on the soul and she begins to flow from heartfelt love. Then the soul loses all its guilt and all its sorrow, and then He begins to teach her His will. Then she begins to taste His sweetness and then He begins to greet her . . . and then He begins to make love to her so that she becomes weak. Then she begins to suck so that He becomes sick with love. . . .

Motion as an Attribute of the Divine

As motion is an essential attribute of the soul's experience within the mystical union, so too is motion an essential attribute of that which the soul seeks, the love of God. The soul seeks freedom in God, and this freedom is described by means of motion imagery. It is not surprising, therefore, that God's love for man is represented as a "miñevlůt" and that his love is consistently characterized as being in motion:

> Der grosse vbervlus gǒtlicher miñe, die niemer stille stat und vlússet jemer me ane vnderlas, ane allerhande arbeit, mit also sůssem vlusse jemer vnverdrossen, dc vnser clein vesselin vol und vbervlússig wirt,—wellen wir es nit

verstopfen mit eigenem willen, so vlússet vnser vesselin jemer úber von gotz gabe. (p. 268)

The great overflowing of divine love that never stops and flows for evermore without pause, without any effort, with such sweet flow ever unflagging, that our little vessel becomes full and overflows,—if we do not stop the flow by our own will, then our vessel will overflow for evermore with the gifts of God.

Constant motion is an attribute not only of God's love but also of God himself. Even when described by means of earth imagery, God does not possess the utter motionlessness that is characteristic of all earth substances. In book 2, using a traditionally mystical image, Mechthild describes God as a mountain—emphasizing primarily the greatness of God as compared to the nothingness of her own soul—but, although the mountain is externally solid and static, it is internally in constant motion:

Einen berg han ich gesehen, ...

Der berg war niden wìs, wolkenvar
Und oben an siner høhin fúrig suñenclar.
Sin begiñen und sin ende konde ich niena finden,
Und biñen spilte er in sich selber
Vliessende goldvar in vnzellicher miñe.

(p. 42)

I have seen a mountain, ...

The mountain was white below, cloud-colored
And above on its heights fiery bright as the sun.
Its beginning and its end I could find nowhere,
And inwardly it swirled and sparkled in itself
Flowing goldhued in inexpressible love.

This concept of God's constant motion is particularly significant in Mechthild's representations of Christ, because in the person of Christ the abstractions of motion and solidity become joined with the paradoxical concept of physical death and spiritual life. Mechthild found this paradox exemplified not only in the Crucifixion and Resurrection but also in the picture of the sleeping Christ child, who though asleep can watch and communicate with the mortals around him :

> In der naht, als gotz sun geboren wart, do wart das kint gesehen in armen tůchern bewunden und mit snůren gebunden . . . . Do sprach ein stiḿe vs dem kinde, es regte doch sinen munt nirgen : Wellent si mich halten in irme gehúgenisse, so wil ich sie halten in minen hulden. (p. 273)

> In the night when God's Son was born, the Child was seen wound in rags and bound with strings. . . . Then spoke a voice from the Child, though His mouth moved not at all: If they will keep Me in their thoughts, then I will keep them in My grace.

The Motion of the Soul within the Mystical Union

Mechthild's emphasis on the motion of God, of his love for man, and of the loving soul within the *unio mystica* seems to underlie the frequent use of music and dancing as images of the mystical union. The relationship of music and dancing to the greater concept of motion as a symbol of the divine has been pointed out at various times as a recurring motif among mystical writers. In her work on Mechthild, Grete Lüers writes :

Die Bewegtheit des Makrokosmos in der Anschauung des Mystikers, die Bewegtheit des Mikrokosmos in seiner eigenen Wesensart sind Charakteristika, die aus den mystischen Texten leicht zu erlesen sind . . . . Diese Bewegung, die die Musik trägt, um derentwillen der mittelalterliche Mensch sie gerade zu schätzen scheint. Alle Musik beruht auf Bewegung . . . und Mechthilds Dichtung ist ein Hauptbeispiel für die Bewegtheit . . . .[2]

The movement of the macrososm in the view of the mystic, the movement of the microcosm in his or her own being are characteristics that are easily selected from the mystical texts. . . . This motion, this dynamics, is . . . the same movement that music conveys, for precisely which reason the medieval person seems to have valued it. All music is based on motion . . . and Mechthild's poetry is a primary example of movement . . . .

In a long passage in book 1 Mechthild portrayed Christ leading the soul in a "lobetantz" ("dance of praise") and the soul says, when Christ tells it to dance:

> Ich mag nit tanzen, herre, du enleitest mich.
> Wilt du das ich sere springe,
> So mŭst du selber voran singen.
> So springe ich in die miñe.
>
> (p. 20)

> I can not dance, Lord, unless You lead me.
> If You want me to leap,
> Then You Yourself must sing,
> Then I will leap into love.

Thus Mechthild connected singing, dancing, and music in general with the *unio mystica*. In a passage quoted earlier in which Mechthild made the word *spil* synonymous with the *unio mystica* ("er wil alleine mit ir spilen ein spil das der lichame nút weis" ["Only with her will He play a game that the body does not know"]), she again linked music with the *unio mystica* by means of a sophisticated play on words. After several lines in which "spil" is used to mean the mystical union, God says to the soul: "Eya liebú tube, din stimme ist ein *seitenspil* [italics added] miner oren; . . ." ("Ah, dear dove, your voice is a *lyre* to my ears") (p. 5), in this way linking music with the union of God and the soul.

Just as the soul as a dancer becomes active only within the *unio mystica,* so does the mystical union represent the opportunity of the soul to move. The soul's potential for motion within the mystical union is represented in a variety of ways by Mechthild. The soul within the body on earth is considered to be of the earth and it is therefore essentially static. Coming in contact with God, however, the soul begins to move as the dancer begins to dance. The soul described as gold is liquified but not destroyed by the fire of God; similarly in one of the most famous of Mechthild's metaphors, the soul is described as wax that is liquified by the fire of God: "Do komen zwo reine nature zesamene, dc heisse fúr der gotheit und dc vliessende wahs der miñenden selen" ("Then come together two pure natures, the hot fire of the divine and the flowing wax of the loving souls") (p. 89). In a later passage Mechthild described an ember that flies out from God and ignites the soul, liquifying it, and through this liquifying process making the earthly soul heavenly:

ein klein vunke har vlúget an die kalten sele, und enpfenget si also vile, das des menschen herze begiñet ze breñende und sin sele ze smelzende und sin ŏgen ze vliessende, so wolte vnser herre gerne einen irdenischen menschen also himelsche machen, das man got werliche mŏhte an ime volgen, miñen und erkeñen; . . . . (p. 187) [3]

a small spark flies out to the cold soul and ignites it so that the human heart begins to burn and the soul to melt and the eyes to flow; thus our Lord wanted to make an earthly human so heavenly that, in her, God might truly be followed, loved, and recognized; . . . .

The *unio mystica* is an opportunity for the soul to shed its earthly stasis and to assume the flowing, liquid motion of God and God's love, or in terms of elemental imagery to lose the attributes of earth and to take on those of the non-static elements. Like the gold and wax in the fire, the soul is still of earth but it has lost the normal properties of its earthly existence.

Images of the Soul as a Bird

One of Mechthild's most frequent images demonstrating the *unio mystica* as a temporary release of the soul from its earthly bonds and as a means for the soul to gain motion and freedom is that of the soul as a bird. At its most obvious, the image of the soul as a bird (an image reinforced by traditional representations of the Holy Spirit as a dove) is merely a traditionally mystical cliché that had originated in the Song of Songs, for example: "O du reinú tube an dinem wesende!" ("O you pure dove in your being!") (p. 10), "Du bist min turteltube an diner súfzunge" ("You are My turtle-dove in your sighing") (p. 16), or:

Eya liebú tube, din fusse sint rot, din vedern sint eben, din mund ist reht, din ŏgen sint schŏne, din hŏbet ist sleht, din wandelunge ist lustlich, din flug ist snel, und du bist alzesnel zŭ der erde. (p. 37)

Ah, dear dove, your feet are red, your feathers are trim, your mouth is true, your eyes are beautiful, your head is smooth, your way is delightful, your flight is fast, and all too quickly you are back to earth.

A second traditional influence on Mechthild's bird imagery, along with that of the Song of Songs and itself in fact a development from the Song of Songs, is the image of the Virgin Mary as a dove. By means of this image are established at different points both the similarity of Mary and the soul ("O tube ane gallen!" ["O dove without gall"] [p. 9], addressed to both Mary and the soul) and the disparity of their relative worth ("Das nam si v́r gut, / Dc dú unedele kra [the soul] bi der turteltube [Mary] stůnt" ["She found it good / That the ignoble crow stood by the turtledove"] [p. 32]).

Mechthild did not, however, restrict herself to traditional descriptions of the soul as a dove or nightingale. At one point she depicted the soul as an eagle, an image more traditionally employed as a symbol of God, Christ, or Saint John.[4] In book 1 Mechthild envisioned the soul's ascent from the earth to God: "Si kumet geswungen als ein are / Usser der tieffi in die hǒhin" ("She comes soaring like an eagle / Out of the depths into the heights") (p. 17). Whether merely implied or stated explicitly, each of these images demonstrates the ability of the soul to free itself, by means of love for God, from the bonds of its earthly existence and to move upward toward God with unfettered motion. Consistent with the general tendencies in the development of Mechthild's style, the bird image is employed in book 7 more didactically than previously but also with unmistakable clarity of meaning:

Dc der vogel lange bi der erden ist, da mitte verbǒset er sine vlúgel und sine vedern werdent swere. So hebet er sich vf in eine hǒhin und weget sine vederen und zúhet sich vf in eine hǒhin also lange, untz er den luft ergriffet, so kumet er in dem vluge. Je lenger er vlúget, je er wuñenklicher swebet, kume als vil dc er dc ertrich beruret dc er sich labe. Also hat ime der miñe vlugel die irdensche wollust benomen, glicher wis sollen wir vns bereiten, alse wir zů sollen komen. (p. 273)

When the bird is long on earth, it thereby spoils its wings and its feathers become heavy. Then it raises itself up high and moves its feathers and pulls itself up high until it catches the wind and then arrives in flight. The longer it flies, the more blissfully it floats, scarcely touching the earth to refresh itself. Thus the wings of love have taken away earthly desire; in the same way we should prepare ourselves if we are to come there.

As is implied by the general image of the bird, the soul must eventually relinquish its mobility and freedom and return to its earthly restraints: "du bist alzesnel zů der erde" ("All too quickly you are back to earth"). The only possibility for eternal release is the death of the body, which would perpetually free the soul from earthly restrictions and gain the soul's admittance to heaven. However, even this permanent union with God does not, according to Mechthild, extinguish the soul's desire for mobility. In a vision of the reception of souls by the Trinity in heaven, Mechthild described the process by which the souls progress through the levels of heaven, creating a picture of exultant, ecstatic motion:

> Der helige geist git ŏch us
> Sinen miñenden himelvlus,
> Damitte er den seligen schenket
> Und si so vollen trenket,
> Dc si mit vrŏden singent,
> Zartelich lachent und springent
> In gezogener wise, und vliessent und swiñent,
> Si vliegent und kliñent
> Von kore ze kore und vúr des riches hŏhin.

(pp. 219–20)

The Holy Spirit also gives of
His loving heavenly river
By His pouring for the blessed,
And they drink their fill
So that they sing with joy,
Lovingly laugh and leap
In a seemly fashion, and flow and swim,
They fly and climb
From choir to choir and come before the
    heights of the realm.

"Sweben" and the Concept of Pure Motion

In describing the souls' ascent through the various levels
of heaven ("von kore ze kore" [from choir to choir]) or,
within the *unio mystica,* the ascent from earth to God,
Mechthild employed words that denote motion with a direc-
tion: *vliessen, swimen, vliegen,* or *klimen,* ("flow," "swim,"
"fly," or "climb") for example. After the soul reaches the
highest level of heaven, the word most frequently employed
is *sweben,* denoting floating, hovering, motion without a
goal, or motion for its own sake. Simultaneously, through
the use of this word, it is implied that one attribute of the
essence of the Trinity is constant, paradoxically directionless
motion.

> Die seligen die nu in dem himel swebent und da so
> wuneklichen lebent, die sint alle beuangen mit einem
> liehte, und sint durchflossen mit einer miñe und sint
> vereinet mit einem willen, ... (p. 59)

The blessed who now float in heaven and live so blissfully
there are all illuminated by one light and are penetrated
by one love and are united by one will, ...

This passage implies that once the soul reaches heaven it no
longer needs to search for God or *vliessen* or *vliegen* toward

God; rather the soul *swebt* and passively lets itself be penetrated (*durchflossen*) by God's love. Similarly in another,
later passage Mechthild refers to "die ewigen menscheit, die
da swebet in der ewigen gotheit, . . ." ("eternal humanity
that floats there in the eternal divinity, . . .") (p. 260) and
again : "Herre, selig sint die ŏgen, / Die das miñesweben
eweklich sont schŏwen" ("Lord, blessed are the eyes / That
shall eternally see the floating of love") (p. 42). These passages make it evident that Mechthild's use of *sweben* has
as a necessary component the concept of eternity. *Vliessen*
and other such goal-oriented verbs represent a temporary
activity of the soul or of God that is ultimately only one
part of the eternal motion of God and his universe. Thus,
Mechthild paradoxically speaks of "die spilende vlŭt, / Die
in der heligen drivaltekeit swebet" ("the swirling flood /
That floats in the holy Trinity") (p. 104). To man, God's love
is a *vlût* but, to God, a *sweben*. One is a temporal manifestation of the other, which is eternal. Therefore, when Mechthild employs the word *sweben* in descriptions of the soul, she
apparently intended to demonstrate the soul's longing for
eternal, passive submission to God's love and will, as is exemplified by two images of the soul as a fish immersing
itself in the water of the Trinity :

> Wŏltistu [God] vliessen so mŏhte si sweben,
> Wan der visch mag uf dem sand nit lange leben
> Und frisch wesen,

> If You were to flow, then she might float,
> For the fish can not be long upon the sand
> And stay alive.

and :

Und si [the soul] sol jemer me in miner heligen drivaltekeit
Mit sele und mit libe sweben und spilen sat
Und ertrinken als der visch in dem mere.

(p. 158)

And in My holy Trinity forevermore shall she
With soul and with body float and delight
And drown as a fish in the sea.

In both instances the fish does not swim in the water but
rather passively lets the water move around it. The soul
must actively seek God but, once having found Him, is
blissfully content to submit passively to a total immersion in
Him.

The Ultimate Stillness of God

In spite of the overwhelming emphasis in *Das fliessende
Licht* on motion as a positive attribute of God, it must be
mentioned that the ultimate end of all this motion is an
absolute stillness:

> Die unendliche Dynamik endet doch letzten Grundes
> in unendlicher Statik: Der giessende, fliessende, schmel-
> zende Gott ist in seiner letzten Wesenheit die ewig
> ruhende Gottheit.[5]

The endless dynamic ultimately ends in endless stasis:
The gushing, flowing, melting God is in His final essence
the eternally resting divinity.

As this stillness applies to God so does it apply to the love
that comes from God and in fact is God ("Das ich dich miñe
dikke, das han ich von nature, wan ich selbe die miñe bin"
["That I love you often comes from My nature, for I Myself
am love"] [p. 13]). Thus Mechthild described the paradox

of love between God and the soul that is all movement, yet simultaneously is utterly still:

> Hienach hat die grosse miñe ir nature, si vlússet nit mit trehnen, mere si breñet in dem grossen hiñelfúre. Da iñe vlússet si allerverrost, und stat in ir selber allerstillost. (p. 109)

> Here is the nature of great love; it does not flow with tears, rather it burns in the great heavenly fire. In the fire it flows the farthest, yet remains in itself the stillest.

This ultimate, eternal stillness of God is not, however, to be identified with the paralytic stillness of the earth or of the soul within the body. The latter is the stillness of involuntary confinement; the former is a stillness that contains within itself, and transcends, all motion. The stasis of the earth is evil because it symbolizes the separation of the soul and God; transcendent stillness is the greatest good because it symbolizes ultimate and perfect union within the godhead.

In this concept of the ultimate motionlessness of God, one finds again the influence of ancient philosophy on Mechthild's thought, for Aristotle had hypothesized that "time is the measure of motion." [6] The mystical paradox of motion and transcendent motionless is a paraphrase of the Aristotelian concept of time and eternity:

> In reality everything in the universe is in flux, and time and movement form a single continuum. . . . It is open to man to seek a certain emancipation from this steady onward flow of time and change and he can do this by achieving through the exercise of his intellect a momentary experience of the timelessness of God Himself. [7]

By extension of this principle then, the things of the earth, represented by earth images in *Das fliessende Licht,* are necessarily transient substances because of their lack of motion. Only that which can move may partake of eternity. Only the essences of fire, air, or water, bearing a potential for movement, can symbolize time, eternity, and the divine.

Notes to Chapter 4

1. "Das metaphorische Verb 'brennen' ist wohl zurückzuführen auf die Identifikation der Gottheit mit Sonne, Licht oder Feuer. . . . Vielleicht liegt der Ursprung in den alten Sonnenreligionen." Lüers, p. 181.

"The metaphorical verb 'to burn' is probably derived from the identification of the divine with sun, light, or fire. . . . Perhaps the origin lies in the old sun religions."
2. Lüers, pp. 110–11.
3. Mechthild's image of the *vunke* resembles but is not identical with the *vunkelin* of Meister Eckhart. The spark of which Mechthild spoke does not actually seem to be a part of the soul, whereas Eckhart's spark is: "that part or faculty of the soul which, or by means of which, the mystical union of the soul with God takes place. It is the seat of conscience and also of the religious consciousness, . . ." *See* James M. Clark, *The Great German Mystics: Eckhart, Tauler and Suso* (Oxford: Basil Blackwell, 1949), pp. 19–20. Nevertheless both the *vunke* and the *vunkelin* seem to have their origins in the sixth-century writings of Pseudo-Dionysius Areopagita as a consequence of Neoplatonic emanation theories. A similar concept is also found in Thomas Aquinas's thirteenth-century discussions of the *scintilla animae*.
4. Gertrude Jobes in *Dictionary of Mythology, Folklore and Symbols*, vol. 1 (New York: The Scarecrow Press, Inc., 1961), p. 483, states: "Saint John is said to be the evangelist who soared to heaven to gaze on the light of immutable truth with keen and undazzled eyes."
5. Lüers, p. 109.
6. Dillistone, p. 82.
7. Dillistone, p. 81.

Liquids and the Nourishment of the Soul

The symbolic properties of liquids, especially the water of baptism and the blood of Christ, are always positive, efficacious, and beneficial to man. Water is a traditional Christian symbol of cleansing, new creation, fertilization, refreshment, and regeneration. These are fundamentally overlapping concepts, each one being a specific form of general, positive transformation. In Mechthild's work, too, liquids symbolize consistently the beneficial effects of God upon the soul; and the nourishment of the soul by God, expressed by means of liquid imagery, is one of the recurring motifs of *Das fliessende Licht*.

Throughout her work Mechthild frequently symbolized the drive or passion of God and the soul for one another as the physical sensations of hunger and thirst. As the water of baptism physically represents God's power to purify spiritually, so do hunger and thirst represent the spiritual stimuli that compel God to man and man to God. Moreover, as the satiation of physical hunger and thirst signifies physical nourishment for the body, so does that which God and man give to each other signify spiritual nourishment.

The reasons for Mechthild's choice of this physical terminology seem to be fairly obvious. There are, to be sure,
various precedents for this type of imagery to be found in
the Bible: in the Song of Songs and also in many other
passages in which man's thirst (longing for God) is quenched
by water (God's grace). These images are especially common
in the Old Testament book of Isaiah and the Gospel of John
in the New Testament:

> I will open rivers in the high hills, and fountains in
> the midst of the plains: I will turn the desert into pools
> of waters, and the impassable land into streams of water.
> (Isaiah 41:18)

> They shall not hunger, nor thirst, neither shall the
> heat nor the sun strike them. For he that is merciful to
> them, shall be their shepherd, and at the fountain of
> waters he shall give them drink. (Isaiah 49:10)

> "He, however, who drinks of the water that I will give
> him shall never thirst; but the water that I will give him
> shall become in him a fountain of water, springing up
> unto life everlasting." (John 4:13–14)

Similar imagery is also found, of course, in the Eucharist
with the drinking of wine and eating of bread as the blood
and body of Christ and in Christ's words to the Apostles at
the Last Supper:

> And I appoint you to a kingdom, even as my Father has
> appointed to me, that you may eat and drink at my table
> in my kingdom . . . . (Luke 22:29–30)

A less obvious reason for the images of physical consumption and nourishment in Mechthild's work, however,
is her belief that the drive of God toward the soul and of the

soul toward God is a natural and necessary spiritual instinct.
As thirst and hunger are natural physical drives, so is for
Mechthild the interdependence of God and the soul a neces-
sary and irresistible spiritual drive.

In her description of God's rationale for the creation of
man, Mechthild represented this creation as a necessary act
because of God's need for a bride to love:

> Do sprach der ewig sun mit grosser zuht: Lieber vat-
> ter, min *nature* sol ŏch frucht bringen. Nu wir wunders
> wellen begiñen, so bilden wir den M. [man] na mir,
> alleine ich grosses jamer vorsihe; ich *mŭs* doch den M.
> eweklich miñen. Do sprach der vatter: Sun, *mich rŭret
> ŏch ein kreftig lust* in miner gŏtlichen brust und ich
> dŏnen al von miñe [italics added]. (p. 69)

> Then the eternal Son spoke with great propriety: Dear
> Father, My nature shall also bear fruit. Now We will
> work wonders and form mankind in My image, even
> though I foresee great sorrow; I must still love mankind
> eternally. Then the Father spoke: Son, a powerful desire
> stirs also in My divine breast and I resound totally with
> love.

Thus, Mechthild considered the creation of man by God
to have occurred because God and, even more so, Christ
were driven by the necessity of love. Christ does not love
man because He so chooses but rather because He must
("ich mŭs) and thus is explained Christ's subjection to the
Crucifixion. God, too, because He is love, has no choice but
to love; love is His nature:

> Das ich dich miñe dikke, das han ich von nature, wan
> ich selbe die miñe bin. Das ich dich sere miñe, das han
> ich von minen gerunge, wañ ich gere das man mich sere
> miñe. Das ich dich lange miñe, das ist von miner ewekeit
> wan ich ane ende bin. (p. 13)

That I love you often comes from My nature, for I Myself
am love. That I love you greatly comes from My desires,
for I desire greatly to be loved. That I love you long
comes from My eternity, for I am without end.

Love is the nature of God, and even God must obey the
commands of His own nature. All creatures act as they are
compelled by their natures, and thus the soul is compelled
to God as God is compelled to the soul:

> Got hat allen creature das gegeben,
> Das si ir nature pflegen;
> Wie môhte ich den miner nature widerstan?
> Ich mûste von allen dingen in got gan,
> Der min vatter ist von nature,
> Min brûder von siner mônscheit,
> Min brútegôm von miñe
> Und ich sîn ane anegenge.
>
> (pp. 21–22)

> God has given to all creatures
> That they follow their own natures;
> How might I then resist my nature?
> I must go away from all things into God
> Who is my Father by nature,
> My Brother by His humanity,
> My Bridegroom by love,
> And I have always been His.

In a later passage Mechthild reiterated this point by equating the soul with a nightingale forced by its nature to sing:

> Die nahtegal
> Die mûs je singen,
> Wan ir nature spilet von miñen al.
> Der ir das beneme, so were si tot.
> Eia grosser herre, bedenke min not.
>
> (p. 27)

> The nightingale
> Must ever sing,
> For its nature overflows with love.
> If anyone were to take that from it,
>   then it would be dead.
> Ah, mighty Lord, consider my need.

Both God and the soul of man have, therefore, a natural desire for each other, a desire that originates from love. God is love and must therefore, from love, desire the soul of man; the soul is created by and bound to God and to love and therefore must desire God.

Because Mechthild considered this mutual desire to be a spiritual instinct, it is understandable that she chose physical equivalents such as hunger and thirst to symbolize it. Thus, the soul, seeking God because of the soul's overwhelming desire for Him, says: "Herre, so beite ich deñe mit hunger und mit durste" ("Lord, thus I abide with hunger and with thirst") (p. 34), and again later: "ich habe nah dem himelischen vatter einen hunger . . . . Und ich han nach sinem sun einen durst" ("I have a hunger for the heavenly Father . . . And I have a thirst for His Son") (p. 64). Mechthild believed moreover that the desire of the soul for God comes from God and that it therefore is an insatiable desire. As God is eternal, so are His love and the soul's desire for Him:

Die v́bersússe gerunge, wuñenklich hungerig, miñenvol,
Die vliessent jemer me in die selen
Vberswenkig von gotte,
Noch deñe behaltet die sele iren sússen hunger
Und lebet ane kumber.

(p. 259)

The sweetest desires, blissfully hungry, full of love,
Flow forevermore into the soul

Superabundantly from God;
Still the soul keeps its sweet hunger
And lives without care.

In a narrow sense Mechthild used the images of hunger and
thirst to describe the soul's need and desire to find God. In
a broader sense, hunger and thirst describe the dilemma of
earthly existence and the importance of free will.

Mechthild demonstrated quite clearly that the desire for
God is the natural function of the soul of man. If man's
being consisted only of the soul, there apparently would be
no sin. no impurity, no turning away from God. The soul of
man is unfortunately chained to his body, however. Because
of this bondage to the flesh, man is subject to sin and impurity. Man is composed of soul and body, and the two are
inherently antagonistic. To feed one is to starve the other.
It is man's free will that must decide whether to seek
nourishment for the body or for the soul, whether to satisfy
physical or spiritual needs. The choice made by man's free
will decides his ultimate fate. According to Mechthild, all
men after the end of their earthly existences must eat and
drink that which they have pursued on earth:

> Dis hat got alsust gemessen:
> Was wir mit uns hinan fûren,
> Das mûssen wir da trinken und essen.

(p. 86)

> For God has made it so:
> What we take along with us
> That must we there drink and eat.

Even though men die, their hunger and thirst are eternal,
and Mechthild believed that eternal hunger and thirst (that
is, spiritual hunger and thirst) can be satisfied only by God.

Those men who satisfy physical desires and neglect spiritual needs on earth still possess, after death, an eternal spiritual hunger. This hunger is insatiable, however, because God is lost to them. Souls in hell hunger and thirst for God, for spiritual nourishment, but they are forced to eat stones and drink pitch and sulphur, the earthly symbols of their earthly sins:

> Die hie [on earth] den v́beratz und den v́bertrank so flisseklich begant, die mŭssent mit ewigem hunger vor Lutzifer stan und essent glúiendige steine. Ir trank ist swebel und bech. (p. 84)

> Those who here so diligently overate and overdrank must stand with eternal hunger before Lucifer and eat glowing stones. Their drink is sulphur and pitch.

The exercising of free will is thus represented as the satiation of hunger and thirst (the use of solid substances signifying corruption and liquids signifying spiritual nourishment). This imagery is found again in a long allegorical passage describing the creation and existence of a creature called *alles nútze* (All Useful):

> Die tier betútet ware geistlich lúte . . . . Dis tier isset nit mere, es hat einen grossen zagel, der ist vol honiges, den suget es alle tage. Es hat ŏch guldine grañe, die klingent also schone als es suget, das im die sŭsse stiñe und der vrŏliche klang spiset in sin herze, und der lip wirt gespiset von des sŭssen honiges trank. . . . Die guldine grañe, das ist die edel gotzmiñe, die dur das miñende herze in die edel sele klinget . . . .
> Das tier hat etweñe ein natúrliche lust, dc es des meres trinke dur einen unnútzen turst, so mag es niemer genesen, es mŭsse das bitter merwasser vslassen und widergeben. Also ist es vmb vns súnder gelegen. Sweñe

wir trinken den pfûl der welte und nútzen dú unedelkeit
vnsers vleisches na dem rate des bôsen geistes; o we! so
ist uns selben mit vns selben vergeben. (pp. 111–12)

The animal signifies truly spiritual people . . . . The animal
no longer eats; it has a large tail filled with honey that it
sucks every day. It also has golden whiskers that chime
beautifully as it sucks so that the sweet voice and the
pleasant chiming nourish its heart, and the body is nourished by the sweet honey drink . . . . The golden whiskers
are the noble love of God that chime through the loving
heart into the noble soul. . . .

Sometimes because of a useless thirst the animal has a
natural desire to drink from the sea from which it might
never recover; it has to spit out and forego the bitter sea
water. Thus it is with us sinners. When we drink the mud
puddle of the earth and follow the baseness of our flesh
on the advice of the evil spirit; oh! then we ruin ourselves.

It is notable that the animal avoids all solid foods; its heart
(that is, soul) is nourished by music from God's love, its
body by the honey from its tail that represents faith. The
animal has a natural thirst that it is tempted to slake by
drinking the bitter sea water. From this passage it is apparent that, although liquids are generally positive substances, they can be tainted by the earth, as sea water is
made undrinkable by the salt and dirt it contains. Like the
pitch and sulphur drunk by the souls in hell, sea water has
liquid form but no nourishing qualities. Thus, Mechthild
distinguished between water falling from heaven (or water
gushing from a spring) and water that stands still and becomes tainted. It is interesting that Mechthild considered
the origins of man to be not in pure water but rather in the
contaminated water of the ocean:

Do sach ich wie dc tier wart gezelet an einem eilande in dem mere von dem schlîme der sich súveret vs dem mere, zwischent der heissen suñen und dem mere. Also dc di suñe wc des tieres vater und dc mer sin mûter und der schlîm sin materie. (p. 111)

Then I saw how the animal was created on an island in the sea from the slime that comes from the sea, between the hot sun and the sea. Thus the sun was the animal's father and the sea its mother and the slime its matter.

Apparently Mechtild considered it man's Christian duty to turn away from his origins (the sea and the slime) because of the taint they bear. Humanity by nature must thirst, but this thirst must be slaked only by a pure liquid representing God (such as the honey) rather than by the polluted water of the sea.

The Consumed and Consuming God

Because Mechthild described the soul's desire for God and God's desire for the soul as hunger and thirst and because the love of God and the soul is often described as liquid, it is consistent that Mechthild should represent the acceptance of God's love or gifts by the soul and of the soul's love by God as drinking. Thus, when the loving soul and God are united in heaven, this union is described as a mutual drinking from one another:

er [wil] in siner ewigen hochgezit selber vs trinken . . . alle die helikeit, die er mit sinem lieben sune in unser sele und in vnser menschlichen sin gegossen hat. [Christ speaks:]
> Ja ich sol trinken vs von dir,
> Und du solt trinken vs von mir,
> Alles dc got gûtes in vns behalten hat.

(p. 204)

At His eternal wedding He will Himself drink all the holiness that He with His beloved Son has poured into our soul and into our human senses.

> Yes I shall drink from you
> And you shall drink from Me
> Everything good that God has preserved in us.

This humanizing of God as a being that physically consumes is found throughout Mechthild's work but is especially common in the early work. In book 1 God tells the soul: "dine worte sint wurtzen minem munde" ("your words are spices to my mouth") (p. 5). And this type of imagery (the consumption of the soul by God) is used by Mechthild to point out the difference in man's existence before and after the expulsion from the Garden of Eden. Before the expulsion humanity had been a "pure food" for God:

> Die sele, die vil reine spise,
> Die inen got hat gelobt in dem paradyse,
> Die solte in grosser helikeit mit irem lichamen bliben.
>
> > (p. 70)

> The soul, the pure food
> That God praised in you in paradise,
> Should stay in great holiness with the body.

More commonly, however, it is God or his gifts that are consumed by the soul rather than the soul by God. Obviously Christ is the food and drink of the soul during Communion, and by extension the church altar is described as God's table:

> Nu wil ich mit vrőden zů gottes tische gân,
> Und ich wil enpfân das selbe blůtige lamp,
> Dc an dem heligen crúze wolte stân, . . .
>
> > (p. 237)

Now I will go with pleasure to God's table,
And I will receive the same bloody lamb
That wanted to hang on the holy cross, ...

Related to this is the personification of God as a "wirt" or host who must feed His hungry guests. Mechthild also envisions God at one point as a divinity who questions whether or not to feed His ungrateful children, the priests. Speaking of these priests taking Communion, God says they

sŏnt min lamp lebendig essen, und sŏnt sin blŭt súfzende trinken, so mŏgen si siner grossen sere reht gedenken. Ist er aber schuldig an im selben, so essent minú kint dc himelbrot und judas vert zŭ der helle. Und ist das gezúge dc da hŏrt zŭ der messe nit vollekomen, so stat der gotz tisch ital und den kinden wirt ire spise benomen. (p. 68)

should eat my lamb alive and should drink His blood with sighs so that they might properly contemplate His great suffering. If one is guilty, however, then My children will eat the bread of heaven, and Judas will go to Hell. And if the propriety that is part of the Mass is not perfect, then the divine table will stand empty and from the children their food will be taken.

The importance of proper preparation by the soul, if it is to benefit from the consumption of God's gifts, is again emphasized in a dialogue in which Love attempts to convince a soul to give itself to God. The soul benefits from God's gifts only if the soul experiences a desire for them:

Miñe : Was hilfet, das man ein schlaffenden man schone
kleidet
Und im edele spise vorsetzet diewile er schlaffet,
So mag er doch nit essen?
Eya liebi mi, lâ die weken.

(p. 45)

Love : What good does it do to dress richly a sleeping man
And to set noble food before him while he sleeps
So that he is unable to eat?
Oh, my love, wake up.

As a result of the necessity of the soul's preparation for
God's gifts, the concept of tasting and of eating and drinking
by the soul becomes a metaphor for the entire mystical
union. The image of consuming God during Communion is
extended by Mechthild to represent the ultimate mystical
experience. One therefore finds passages such as the following in which the soul's experience of God is a spiritual
drinking or tasting of Him : "Mir smekket nit, wan alleine
got, / Ich bin wunderliche tot" ("Nothing tastes good to me
but God alone, / I am wondrously dead") (p. 104), or :

Owe ich dir in dem homûte lihte entwenke.
Mere, je ich tieffer sinke,
Je ich sûsser trinke.

(p. 107)

Ah, in my pride how easily I am untrue to You.
Rather, the more deeply I sink,
The more sweetly I drink.

The soul hungers and thirsts for God alone, and God can at
will satiate the hunger and slake the thirst of the soul :

Der vngeteilet got spiset si
Mit dem blikke sines heren antlútes
Und fúllet si mit dem unlidigen ateme
Sines vliessenden mundes.

(p. 28)

The undivided God feeds her
With the glance of His lordly countenance

And fills her with the irresistible breath
Of His flowing mouth.

It is consistently emphasized that this nourishing of the
soul by God occurs entirely at the whim of God, even
though God is compelled by His nature to love and therefore to nourish the soul. The soul can only request; God
alone may grant:

> ich bitte in vil gerne
> Dc er mir vfschliesse
> Die spilende vlût,
> Die in der heligen drivaltekeit swebet,
> Da die sele alleine von lebet.

(p. 104)

> I gladly bid Him
> Open to me
> The swirling flood
> That floats in the holy Trinity;
> The soul lives from this alone.

Only when the soul, after the death of the body, reaches
heaven and attains eternal union with God will the needs
of the soul be satisfied freely and eternally by God. This
eternal union is described by Mechthild as a banquet for
the soul that the soul has earned by earthly need: "Dis
spricht vnser herre: Man sol des kúnges spise nit vergeben
hin setzen, ê man die irdenschú notdurft wol habe gessen"
("Our Lord says this: The king's food should not be set
forth in vain before earthly necessity has been eaten") (p.
187). Thus physical or earthly need can paradoxically be
eaten by and is nourishment for the soul. Once the soul has
nourished itself by earthly hunger and thirst, then the
eternal feast is served to the soul by Christ in heaven:

Sweñe die edelen gerihte sint geschehen,
Da Jesus Christus selber dienen wil,
So sihet man da den allerhôhesten lobetanz.

(p. 252)

When the noble dishes are placed
Where Jesus Christ Himself will serve,
Then will be seen the highest dance of praise.

Because the love relationship of God and the soul is an interacting one, rather than a mere acting upon the soul by God, there is found in *Das fliessende Licht* a consuming of the soul and a taking of nourishment from the soul by God. Because Mechthild considered the gifts of God to the soul to be immeasurably greater than the gifts of the soul to God and because she was more concerned with the soul's experience of God than with God's experience of the soul, the occurrences of images showing God's nourishment by the soul are relatively infrequent. Such references are to be found, however, even when God's dependence on the soul is merely implied, as it is in the following passage:

Den si [die miltekeit] was gibet die danken des gotte
Mit heliger iñekeit, der bevindet des herzen stat
Als dc edel tranke in reine vas.

(p. 251)

Those to whom she (generosity) gives thank God for it
With holy fervor; He finds the place of the heart
To be a noble drink in a pure vessel.

The soul serves as a container for love from which God nourishes Himself. More explicit is a passage in which Christ sucks nourishment from the heart of the soul (emphasizing the parallel between the soul and Mary, the prototypical loving soul):

Do gieng die arme dirne [Mechthild] zů dem altar mit grosser liebe und mit offenen sele. Do nam sant Johañes dc wisse lamp mit sinen roten wunden, und leit es in den kŏwen irs mundes. Do leite sich dc reine lamp uf sin eigen bilde in iren stal, und sŏg ir herze mit sinem sůssen munde. Je me es sŏg, je me si es im gonde. (p. 33)

Then the poor girl went to the altar with great love and with an open soul. Then Saint John took the white lamb with its red wounds and laid it in her mouth. Then the pure lamb lay down upon its own image in her stall and sucked her heart with its sweet mouth. The more it sucked, the more she gave to it.

God or Christ is never represented as eating a solid substance of the soul. That which the soul gives for the nourishment of God is always a liquid as is consistent with Mechthild's depiction of love as fluid. Similarly, although the soul both hungers and thirsts for God and both eats and drinks Him and His gifts, the only nonliquid substance that can serve as nourishment for the soul is the body of Christ or the bread that symbolizes Christ's body. These sanctified solids are exceptions to the general tendency for the soul to feed itself only with fluids, a tendency epitomized by the allegorical animal "alles nútze," which refuses solid food and takes its sustenance from the honey that flows from its tail.

Liquids represent forms of love, either of God for man, of man for God, or of man for man. Mechthild perceived a gradation in relative value between the various forms of love and thus also between various liquids. In a long chapter in book 1 Mechthild depicted a dialogue between the Loving Soul and the Senses ("siñe") in which the Senses suggest various liquids that the Soul might use to refresh itself after the heat of dancing. The senses first suggest the tears of Mary Magdalene, but the Soul replies:

Seele: Swigent, ir herren, ir wissent nit alle was ich meine.
Lant mich ungehindert sin;
Ich wil ein wenig trinken den vngemengeten win.

Sine: In der martyrer blůte mǒgent ir vch sere kůlen.
Seele: Ich bin gemartert so manigen tag,
Dc ich dar nu nit komen mag.

Sine: Frowe, went ir v́ch minekliche kůlen
So neigent v́ch in der juncfrǒwen schos
Ze dem kleinen kint, und sehent und smekent,
Wie der engel frǒde von der ewigen maget
Die unnatúrlichen milch sǒg.
Seele: Dc ist ein kintlich liebi,
Das man kint sǒge und wiege;
Ich bin ein vollewachsen brût,
Ich wil gan nach minem trût.

(pp. 20–21)

Soul: Silence, my lords, you do not know what I mean.
Leave me unhindered;
I want to drink a little of the undiluted wine.

Senses: In the blood of the martyrs you might cool yourself.
Soul: I am martyred so many times
That I can not go that way.

Senses: Lady, if you want to cool yourself with love
Then bend down to the virgin's lap
To the little child and see and taste,
As the joy of the angels sucked
The unnatural milk from the eternal maid.
Soul: That is a childlike love
To suckle and cradle a child;
I am a full-grown bride,
I want to go to my groom.

Although many liquids are sanctified because they represent a type of love, the finest liquid is pure wine, "den vngemengeten win" ("the undiluted wine"), which represents the direct and immediate interaction or love of God and the loving soul. Tears, blood, and milk are all offered as refreshment for the soul. These liquids, however, can not satisfy the thirst of the soul, which instinctively craves the ultimate liquid of divine love, the pure wine of God.

6

The Manifestations of Liquids in *Das fliessende Licht*

The imagery of liquids in Mechthild's work has its primary origins in the significance assigned to liquids in the Christian tradition and in the common medieval conception of a universe composed of four primary elements. According to the medieval cosmological system all existing substances would be classified according to their primary attributes, and all substances of any elemental group would be considered to possess inherent similarities. Thus heat from the sun and heat from a burning candle would both be identified as forms of the element fire; both wind and fog would be identified as forms of the gaseous element air. Most importantly for Mechthild's imagery, there would exist an implicit similarity of all liquid substances—water, blood, wine, milk, or honey—because of the obvious identity of their primary physical characteristic, fluidity.

The symbolic meaning of a substance is often directly

related to its physical attributes. Therefore, if two or more substances have similar physical properties, it is logical that they should also have similar symbolic qualities. It is understandable, therefore, that there exists in Das *fliessende Licht* an identification of liquid substances. Blood, milk, wine, honey, tears, gall, and various forms of water are related, physically and symbolically, because of their common fluidity.

The Ambiguity of Water

In general the positive potential of water seems to be directly related to the purity and motion that it possesses. In spite of the predominantly beneficial significance of water, it also represents at times negative aspects of man's earthly existence. This aspect of Mechthild's water imagery is seen primarily in the significance she ascribed to sea water. This form of water, which represents both the origins of man and also his potential to be destroyed either by God or by the forces of evil, is at one point envisioned as the primordial ocean upon which the earth floats as an island: "dis ertrich swebet vf dem mere" ("this earth floats on the sea") (p. 29). More important, Mechthild made an analogy in book 4 linking the earth and the sea as environments equally menacing to man; in a description of a vision of Enoch and Elias, Mechthild wrote: "Do si dc ertrich angesehent, so erschrekent si, als die man tůnt, die dc mer ansehent, und sich vǒrhtent wie si ϋberkommen sǒllent" ("When they see the earth they are frightened, as people are who see the ocean and worry how they should get across") (pp. 126–27). Moreover, Mechthild pictured herself in another passage as drinking the polluted water of the world ("der welte wasser"), instead of the pure water that flows from God:

O herre, du schonest alzesere mines pfůligen kerkers,
Da ich iñe trinke der welte wasser
Und isse mit grosser jamerkeit
Den eschekůchen miner brŏdekeit, ...

(p. 50)

O Lord, You are too sparing of my muddy prison
Where I drink the water of the world
And eat with great lamenting
The ashcake of my debility, ...

The water of the earth may nourish the body of man, but it contaminates the purity of the soul. These manifestations of water are seldom mentioned by Mechthild. Sea water, the polluted water of the earth, and two liquids originating in the apple of the Tree of Knowledge are the only non-beneficial liquids to be found in Mechthild's work, and they are mentioned only fleetingly. Liquids are, with these exceptions, beneficial to the soul of man.

In connection with Cirlot's statement that water is the transitional element between the ethereal elements and the solid element earth, it is noteworthy that Mechthild showed water to be present in all the levels of creation except the highest and the lowest, heaven and hell. Water is found on earth, in purgatory (for example, souls bathing in tears [p. 36]), and in paradise : "Snellú wasser vliessent da durch und sudenwind zů norden. Do begegente in den wasseren irdenschú sůssekeit getempert mit himelscher wuñe" ("Swift waters flow through it and winds from south to north. In the waters mingled earthly sweetness with heavenly bliss") (p. 270). In heaven, however, water is not mentioned; and in hell the souls who thirst drink not true liquids, but rather liquefied solids, "swebel und bech" ("sulphur and pitch") (p. 84). Water therefore can be viewed as a symbol of hope, which is, in effect, a form of divine grace. Water is totally absent in hell, because of the utter hopelessness of damned souls. Similarly water is absent in heaven because heaven represents the fulfillment of hope rather than hope itself. This hypothesis reinforces Mechthild's conception of motion: motion is found only in the intermediate levels of existence. The earth possesses the stasis of confinement; God, on the other hand, is ultimately and transcendently motionless. Viewed in this way, water represents mediation, transition, and hope. By showing an absence of liquids, Mechthild portrayed both hell, the realm of Lucifer, and also her poetic conception of hell-on-earth, an entirely physical existence of man without God and without hope of salvation.

Although water was most often employed by Mechthild to signify the gifts of God to the soul, she also at times used water as a metaphor for the soul itself. This representation of the soul seems to have arisen from her idea of the origin of the soul. She described the creation of the soul as a flowing out of the inexhaustible divine spring or fountain: "Eya ewiger bruñe der gotheit, da ich vsgevlossen bin . . ." ("Oh, eternal spring of the divine from which I flowed . . .") (p. 116). Because the soul flowed from the spring, it is natural to find a description of the soul as water. Within the *unio mystica* there is found an interaction of God and the soul that Mechthild at times described as the interaction of fire and water: "die spilende suñe der lebendigen gotheit / Schinet dur dc clare wasser der vrólichen menscheit" ("The swirling sun of the living divinity / Shines through the clear water of happy humanity") (p. 104). Similarly the soul is described as a brook that cools the passionate heat of God: "Du bist . . . ein bach miner hitze" ("You are . . . a brook for My heat") (p. 10).

More common than these metaphors of the soul as water, however, are images of water as the substance for which man thirsts. Here again water can represent either good or evil. Man alone of all God's creatures possesses free will: "und ich [God] gibe dir [man] . . . vrien willekore. Liep vor allen liebe, nu sich dich eben wislich vor" ("and I give you . . . free will. You beloved before all others, now prudently take care") (p. 70). Man must choose whether to satiate the thirst of the soul or of the body, whether to drink the clear and flowing water from God or the still and polluted water of the earth. For Mechthild the choice that man should make is obviously the water from God that nourishes the soul. To describe the negative effect of drinking the water of earth, Mechthild contrasted the concepts of drinking ("trinken") and drowning ("ertrinken"). The soul may "drink" the water of God but will "drown" in the water of the earth:

Ist aber sin [man's] herzė offen gegen der welte,

So kunt der bitter nort wint der girekeit
Der welte von vnsern magen,
Das si vns vil klagen,
Dc si des pfûles alze kleine haben,
Da si doch leider iñe versinkent,
Und in den súnden ertrinkent.

(p. 271)

If however his heart is open to the world,

Then comes the bitter north wind of the world's
Covetousness from our families
Who complain to us
That they have too little of the mud puddle
Into which they are sinking,
And they drown in their sins.

The soul that seeks the water of God, however, cannot

perish but rather finds eternal bliss (again expressed by the use of the word *ertrinken*):

Und si [the soul] sol jemer me in miner heligen drivaltekeit
Mit sele und mit libe sweben und spilen sat
Und ertrinken als der visch in dem mere.

(p. 158)

And she forevermore with soul and with body
Shall float and play until content in My holy Trinity
And drown as the fish in the sea.

Water signifying divine grace is so beneficial for the soul that the soul can not perish, but rather exists as a creature that has found its true home. This image of the soul as a fish is found repeatedly as one manifestation of a general tendency by Mechthild to describe man and the soul of man by means of animal images. As it is in the passage above, the fish image usually demonstrates the utter joy of the soul in God and the soul's need for God; an analogy is made between the soul without God and a fish out of water: "der visch mag uf dem sand nit lange leben / Und frisch wesen" ("the fish can not be long upon the sand / And stay alive") (p. 55). Fish imagery is also employed for other purposes, however. Mechthild described souls in purgatory as fish in fiery water, implying that the bliss of heaven (that is, cool water) has not yet been granted to these souls: "Des ist lang dc ich ein vegfúr sach, dc was gelich eim fúrigen wasser. . . . In dem wasser swebten geistliche vische . . ." ("Long ago I saw a purgatory that was like a fiery water . . . . In the water floated spiritual fish") (p. 141). More interesting still is the use of this image to demonstrate the temptation of the soul by the things of earth. Mechthild described a soul existing in the water of God who is tempted by the attractiveness of a piece of red meat but who does not perceive the hook hidden in the meat. It is significant that here again flesh is used to represent the things of earth; flesh itself is not necessarily evil, but it does bring evil with it:

> Der visch in dem wassere der sihet
> Mit grosser ger dc rote as an,
> Damitte man in wil vâhn;
> Er sihet aber nit den angel.
> Also ist es vmb der welte vergift,
> Si bekeñet ires schaden nit.

(p. 242)

> The fish in the water regards
> With great longing the red bait
> With which it would be caught,
> But it does not see the hook.
> Thus it is with the world's poison,
> It does not reveal its harmfulness.

Dew and Rain

The water in which the soul as a fish exists is the divine grace that flows from the spring of the Trinity. Because of Mechthild's concept of the relative physical positions of heaven and earth (that is, heaven lies upward from earth, above the spheres of water, air, and fire) it is only natural that one of the most frequent representations of divine grace should be water that falls from above, as dew or rain. This image is particularly appropriate for Mechthild's purposes because rain falls from above the earth and is, therefore, untainted by contact with the earth. Thus, rain and dew (Mechthild ascribed to dew the same origins and qualities as rain) epitomize both the purity and motion that characterize God and divine grace.

In one passage Mechthild described the earthly existence

of man as a barren field that can be regenerated, nourished, and made fertile by a combination of rain, sun, and dew as three forms of the godhead:

> Herre, min irdensch wesen stat vor minen ŏgen,
> Gelich einem dúrren akker,
> Da wenig gûtes uffe ist gewahsen.
> Eya sûsser Jesu Christe,
> Nu sende mir den sûssen regen diner menscheit,
> Und die heisse suñen diner lebendiger gotheit
> Und den milten towe des heligen geistes,
> Dc ich verclage min herzeleit.
>
> (p. 100)

> Lord, my earthly being stands before my eyes
> Like a barren field
> Where little that is good has grown.
> Ah, sweet Jesus Christ,
> Now send me the sweet rain of Your humanity
> And the hot sun of Your living divinity
> And the mild dew of the Holy Spirit
> So that I may plead the sorrow of my heart.

In this passage dew and rain represent God in his general relationship to the soul. In another passage, however, this same imagery is employed more specifically as a representation of God within the *unio mystica:* "Ich kum zů miner lieben / Als ein tŏwe vf den blůmen" ("I come to My love / As a dew upon the flowers") (p. 9).

In another context the flower that is covered by the dew is not the individual soul but rather the Virgin Mary. In the union of God and the soul, the result of the union is left unexpressed; in the union of God and Mary, however, the union of dew and flower bears the fruit that is Christ. The union of God and the soul occurs only in the spiritual realm. The union of God and Mary, on the other hand, occurs in both spiritual and physical realms. It is a union of purest spirit (God) and purest flesh (Mary) and the fruit of the union is God and man, paradoxically and simultaneously mortal and immortal, an untainted union of spirit and flesh:

> Der sússe tŏwe der vnbeginlicher drivaltekeit hat sich gesprenget vs dem bruñen der ewigen gotheit in den blǔmen der vserwelten maget, und des blǔmen fruht ist ein vntŏtlich got, und ein tŏtlich mensche und ein lebende trost des ewigen liebes, und vnser lŏsunge ist brútegŏm worden. (p. 11)

The sweet dew of the fathomless Trinity has sprung from the spring of the eternal divinity into the flower of the chosen maid, and the fruit of the flower is an immortal God and a mortal human and a living solace of eternal love and our salvation has become bridegroom.

With this image Mechthild created a metaphorical triad of dew, flower, and fruit as an analogy to the holy triad of God, Mary, and Christ, or father, mother, and son. This triad is invoked frequently, for example:

> O grosser tŏ der edelen gotheit!
> O kleine blǔme der sǔssen maget!
> O nútze fruht der schŏnen blǔmen!
>
> Da solt du, herre, din gnade ingiessen,
> So mag ich von diner miñe vliessen.
>
> (p. 144)

> O great dew of the noble divinity!
> O small flower of the sweet maid!
> O useful fruit of the lovely flower!
>
> There, Lord, You should pour Your grace;
> Thus I can flow out of love for You.

The aspect of the union of God and Mary that seems to
have been most appealing to Mechthild is Mary's immaculateness. Mary represents untainted flesh, and she retains
her immaculateness during the conception and the physical
birth of Christ: "und Jesus gieng dur dinen lip als der tŏwe
dur di blůme, also dc dinú kúscheit nie wart berůret" ("and
Jesus went through your body as the dew through the flower
so that your purity was never touched") (p. 65). It is interesting that in this passage Christ is not the fruit of the union
but rather has Himself become the dew. Curiously too,
Mary, in another passage, seems to be symbolized as the
dew (as the soul was represented as clear water) through
which God shines as the sun. This image occurs in a passage
in which Mechthild pondered at great length Mary's reten-
tion of purity. The emphasis on the word *vleisch* leaves no
doubt that Mechthild intended a physical as well as a
spiritual union:

> Do trat dú ganze helige drivaltekeit mit der gewalt
> der gotheit und mit dem gůten willen der menscheit, und
> mit der edeln gevůgheit des heligen geistes dur den
> ganzen lichamen ires magtůmes in der vúrigen sele irs
> gůten willen, und saste sich in das offen herze ires
> allerreinosten vleisches und vereinete sich mit allem dem
> das er an ir vant, also das ir vleisch sin vleisch wart, also
> dc er ein vollekomen kint wůchs in irme libe und also,
> dc si ware můter wart sines vleisches und ein unverseret
> maget bleip . . . .
> Der almehtige got mit siner wisheit, der ewige sun
> mit siner menschlichen warheit, der helig geist mit siner
> cleinlichen sůssekeit, ging dur dú ganzen want Marien
> lichamen mit swebender wuñe ane alle arbeit. Das wc
> also schier geschehen, als die suñe gibet iren schin nach
> dem sůssen tŏwe in miñenklicher růwe. (p. 148)

Then the entire holy Trinity with the force of the
divine and with the good will of humanity and with the

dignity of the Holy Spirit entered into the entire body of her maidenhood in the fiery soul of her good will and sat down in the open heart of her most pure flesh and was united with everything that He found in her so that her flesh became His flesh, that He, a perfect child, grew in her body and that she became true mother of His flesh yet remained an undamaged maiden. . . .

Almighty God with His wisdom, the everlasting Son with His human truth, the Holy Spirit with His delicate sweetness went through all the coverings of Mary's body effortlessly with floating bliss. It happened as swiftly as the sun shines on the sweet dew in loving repose.

While dew at different times represents God, Christ, and even Mary, the image of the fruit is applied only to Christ. The image seems to have been for Mechthild an apt one, representing a union of solid and liquid substances; of flesh and spirit; of God, the purest of liquids, and of Mary, the purest of solids. Christ as "fruht" is a formula image that is often used by Mechthild without any great explicit significance. The concept of fruit as the result of the union of pure liquid and solid images does, however, help to explain certain images such as the one that follows in which the Trinity is a tree and Christ is an apple : "Und da neigen ich dir den hohsten bŏn miner heligen drivaltekeit, / So brichest du dene die grŭnen, wissen, roten ŏpfel miner sanftigen menscheit, . . ." ("And I will bend down to you the highest branch of My holy Trinity, / Then you will pluck the green, white, red apples of My gentle humanity, . . . (p. 51).

Although Mechthild usually employed the images of dew and rain to represent forms of divine grace, in book 1 the image of dew represents the seclusion or the spiritual state that is a necessary prerequisite for the mystical union. The Loving Soul is told by the Senses ("die Siñe") that

Christ as a prince will come to her *with* the dew rather than *as* the dew:

> Des morgens in dem towe, dc ist die besclossen iñekeit,
> Die erst in die sele gât.

> Der fúrste wil vch gegen komẽn
> In dem tŏwe und in dem schŏnen vogelsange.

(p. 19)

> In the morning in the dew is the secret intimacy
> That first goes into the soul.

> The prince will come to you
> In the dew and with the lovely singing of the birds.

This significance ascribed to the dew is more abstract than the simple representation of God as dew or rain, and this type of significance is found much less frequently in Mechthild's work. More commonly, images of water and liquids represent that which comes to the soul from God rather than that which brings the soul to God; they are tangible signs of God's love for humanity.

Blood

As water falling from heaven represents a manifestation of God's love, blood also represents this because of its association with the Crucifixion of Christ. The similarity of the symbolic attributes of water and blood would have arisen from the covenantal significance of both, from their elemental identity as forms of the element water, and from the presence of both during the Crucifixion. In the *New Catholic Edition* of the Bible there is appended to the passage describing the piercing of Christ's side (John 19:34) a footnote that explains the miraculous significance of both the water and the blood that flowed together from the wound:

> this phenomenon was considered a miracle by Origen. The Fathers generally see in it a deeper meaning: the sacred mysteries issuing from the side of Christ, the birth of the Church as Eve was taken from the side of Adam, and so forth.

Thus, in addition to medieval scientific explanations of the similarity of water and blood, there also existed within the patristic tradition of allegorical exegesis a similar justification for Mechthild's symbolic use of the two substances.

Moreover, because of the sanctity attributed to Christ's blood, there is also found in Mechthild's work a more general sanctification of almost all blood. All the water of the Jordan is sanctified by Christ's baptism, and all Christian effort and suffering are ennobled by the effort and suffering of Christ:

> Von der edelen arbeit vnsers herren und von seiner heligen pine ist vnser cristanlichú arbeit und vnser gûtwilligú pine geedelt und geheliget, ze glicher wis als allú wasser sint geheliget von dem Jordane, da vnser lieber herre iñe getöffet wart. (p. 247)

> By the noble work of our Lord and by His holy pain are our Christian work and our goodwilled pain dignified and sanctified in the same way as all waters are sanctified by the Jordan in which our dear Lord was baptized.

The logical extension of this idea is that all Christian blood is sanctified by the blood of Christ. That it is not solely the blood of Christ that is sanctified is seen in a passage in which Mechthild indicated how to effect a cleansing of the medieval Church of its impurity and evil. Mechthild had God say that the Church can be cleansed by its own blood:

Si ist ŏch vnvletig an der húte, wel rat sol ir deñe werden?
Do sprach vnser herre: Ich wil si weschen in ir selbes
blůte . . . . (p. 167)

Her skin is also unclean; what advice shall be given to
her? Then our Lord spoke: I will wash her in her own
blood.

Paradoxically, in spite of the fact that Mechthild considered the noblest forms of water to be those that have
had no contact with the earth, blood is sanctified although
it is of the earth. Mechthild seemed to consider all blood,
even the blood of Christ, to have originated on earth. At
one point she wrote that Christ's blood was a part of Him
given to Him not by God or by the Holy Spirit but by Mary
along with His body: "Gabriel fůrte den namen Jesus mit
dem grůsse alleine hernider. Im war weder bein, noch
vleisch, noch blůt mitte gegeben" ("Gabriel carried the name
Jesus down with the greeting. He was at the same time
given neither bone nor flesh nor blood") (p. 108). At other
times, however, she seemed to contradict this viewpoint,
as she did in the following passage in which the adjective
himelsch is applied to the word *blůt:* "Der ware gottes grůs
/ Der da kunt von der himelschen blůt" ("The true greeting
of God / Comes from the heavenly blood") (p. 40). Whether
or not blood is of the earth, it does not seem to possess the
clinging impurity that is characteristic of solid substances
and the flesh. Thus, for Mechthild, blood is an earthly symbol of God's love and grace, and this symbolic significance
of blood is extended by Mechthild so that Christ's blood is
also employed as a metaphor for her own work. As in the
passages in which she described her work as a "vliessen"
from God, so too did she at one point describe *Das fliessende
Licht* as the heartblood of Christ: "Ich sage dir werlich,

sprach unser herre, in disem bûche stat min herzeblůt geschriben, dc ich in den jungesten ziten anderwarbe giessen wil" ("I tell you truly, spoke our Lord, in this book is written My heart's blood that I will pour again at the Last Judgment") (p. 167).

As the blood of Christ represents God's love for man, so conversely can the blood of man represent man's love for God. Because of this identification of blood and divine love, Mechthild used blood imagery to describe the interaction of God and the soul within the *unio mystica:*

> Alsust, herre: Din blůt und min ist ein vnbewollen,
> Din miñe und minú ist ein vngeteilet,
> Din kleit und min ist ein vnbevleket,
> Din munt und miner ist ein vnkúst etc.
>
> (p. 52)

> Thus, Lord: Your blood and mine is one, immaculate;
> Your love and mine is one, undivided;
> Your dress and mine is one, unsoiled;
> Your mouth and mine is one, unkissed.

In spite of the metaphorical intermingling of the blood of God and man as a symbol of the mystical union, there nevertheless exists a qualitative difference between these forms of blood. Blood in general attains symbolic value for Mechthild in proportion to its significance as an indicator of love. As no man can love so profoundly, so unselfishly, so eternally as Christ, so is the blood of Christ infinitely more valuable than human blood. Similarly, as some persons exhibit a greater capacity for spiritual love than do others, so too is there a qualitative difference attributed to the various forms of human blood. In the following passage Mechthild distinguished among three forms of blood and among the distinctive beneficial powers of each:

Von drier hande blůte seite mir vnser herre alsust: Das erste blůt, das Abel und dú kint, Johañes Baptista und alle die ir helig unschuldiges blůt gussen vor der marter vnsers herren, dc was cristi blůt, wan si litten dur sine liebi den seligen tot. Das ander blůt das was des himelschen vatter blůt, das cristus us sinem vnschuldigen herzen gos. Das dritte blůt, dc man vor dem jungesten tage giessen sol in cristanem gelŏben, dc ist des heligen geistes blůt, wan sunder des heligen geistes andaht wart nie gůttat vollebraht. Der martrer blůt dur cristum, dc gibet geselle-schaf und kůñe; des vatters blůt in cristo git lŏsunge und gelŏben. Das jungest blůt in dem heligen geiste git behaltunge und ere. (pp. 167–68)

Of three types of blood our Lord told me the following: The first blood, that of Abel and the children, John the Baptist and all others who poured their holy, innocent blood before the martyrdom of our Lord, was Christ's blood for they suffered blessed death for the sake of His love. The second blood was the heavenly Father's blood that Christ poured from His innocent heart. The third blood, that shall be poured at the Last Judgment in Christian faith, is the blood of the Holy Spirit for without the devotion of the Holy Spirit no good deed was ever done. The martyrs' blood for the sake of Christ gives community and courage; the Father's blood in Christ gives redemption and faith. The last blood in the Holy Spirit gives protection and honor.

Moreover, the relative values of the blood of Christ and human blood are seen in a description of the Day of Judgment when Christ's blood will be weighed against the total of all the blood shed for Christ by humanity:

Der megde blůt von nature, der martrer blůt dur den cristanen gelŏben und ander man manschlahtige blůt, das ane schult geschihet in rehter not, das wil der helige gotz sun mit sinem blůte wegen, wan es ist in warer vnschult

vs geben. Dc rehte blůt kunt nit in die wage? Warvmbe?
Es ist vor bewollen, aber es lǒschet dieselben súnden, die
da kunt von des vleisches kúnde. (p. 131)

The maidens' blood by nature, the martyrs' blood for the
sake of Christian faith and other types of blood that
occurred innocently in true need, these the holy Son of
God weighs with His blood for it was shed in true inno-
cence. Real blood does not come onto the scales? Why?
It is innately impure, but it does take away those sins that
come from the knowledge of the flesh.

It is apparent in these passages and others that for
Mechthild blood attains sanctity only by being shed for
someone else. Any physical blood may be used to cleanse
the sins of the flesh, but only blood innocently shed may be
placed in balance with the blood of Christ. This is one
indication, verified by other ideas in Mechthild's work,
that blood is a symbol of love because it is, more specifically,
a symbol of suffering. As Christ suffered for the sake of His
love for humanity, so must humanity endure suffering as a
sign of its love for Christ or God. Blood, because of its
association with the Passion of Christ, is representative less
of physical life than it is of the sacrificing of physical life.
It signifies, both in Christ and men, the enduring of suffering
for the sake of another. The blood that Mechthild considered to be sanctified is not blood in its natural state;
blood *within* the body is inefficacious. Blood attains spiritual
value only by being shed innocently and for the sake of
another being.

Even as baptismal water gained sanctity only after the
baptism of Christ, it seems, too, that the suffering of mankind and the shedding of human blood gained spiritual
worth only after the Crucifixion of Christ. Mechthild implied that, although humanity had suffered and bled before

Christ, human blood had been worthless because it was not shed from love. Before Christ, human blood and wounds had represented merely a useless suffering that humanity had brought upon itself by the expulsion from the Garden of Eden. One of the miracles of Christ's existence was the spiritual utility that He had brought to the sufferings of Christian humanity. Through Christ, these sufferings were no longer self-inflicted and self-serving but rather were a visible sign of human self-sacrifice for the sake of Christ and God. Before Christ, the physical wounds of mankind represented also a spiritual wounding; after Christ, physical wounds represent spiritual healing, purification, and salvation:

> Eya, do knúwete der ewig sun vor sinem vatter und sprach: Lieber vatter, ... Ich wil gerne die blûtigen menscheit an mich nemen und ich wil des M [enschen] wunden salben mit dem blûte miner vnschulde und wil alles menschen sere verbinden mit einem tûche der ellenden smacheit untz an min ende, und ich wil dir, trut vatter, des M. schulde mit menschlichem tode vergelten. (p. 71)

> Ah, then the eternal Son knelt down before His Father and spoke: Dear Father, ... I will gladly take bleeding humanity upon Myself and I will anoint humanity's wounds with the blood of My innocence and will bind well all humanity with a cloth of humility until My end, and I will repay to You, beloved Father, humanity's guilt by a human death.

Christ suffered and bled for mankind. Humanity's duty is to emulate Christ (*imitatio Christi*), to suffer and bleed in order to demonstrate love for Christ and for God. Humanity is made of both flesh and blood, and both must be sacrified to God: "die geistlichen lúte oppferent got in sinem dienste

ir vleisch und ir blůt, . . ." ("spiritual people sacrifice to God
in His service their flesh and their blood, ...") (p. 233).
Sanctity is not inherent in either the flesh or the blood of
humanity; it is earned by sacrificing them for the sake of
God, by the wounding of one's flesh and by the shedding
of one's blood. Thus, in a passage such as "die kůne marterer,
die die himelstrasse mit irme blůt begossen hant" ("the cour-
ageous martyrs who have sprinkled the road to heaven with
their blood") (p. 155), it is clear that blood represents the
physical suffering and self-sacrifice that bring the martyrs
to heaven. Blood and wounds symbolize suffering and
sacrifice that in turn symbolize the love relationship between
God and the soul. This is evident in a number of passages
in which Mechthild prayed not to God or Christ but rather
to the divine wounds and suffering:

> O blůtigú not,
> O wunden tief, o smerze gros!
> La mich herre nit verderben
> In aller miner pinen not. Amen.
>
> (p. 234)

> O bloody need,
> O deep wounds, o great pain!
> Do not let me perish, Lord,
> In all my need. Amen.

Precisely this paradoxical concept of spiritual life
through physical death, of spiritual nourishment through
physical need, of spiritual happiness through physical suffering, gave rise to the preoccupation with the wounds, blood,
and suffering of Christ that is so often found in the religious
art of the late Middle Ages. Mechthild also showed this
preoccupation but, for the most part, only in her later work.
In the early books her descriptions of Christ and His

physical appearance portray Him as a handsome, un-blemished youth, and Mechthild made frequent erotic references to His hands, face, eyes, and mouth. In the later books, reflecting a change in the nature of Mechthild's mysticism, the references to Christ's appearance dwell extensively on the wounds of His hands and feet and on the blood that flows from the wounds. In book 1 the divine bridegroom is described in this way:

> Vide mea sponsa: Sich wie schône min ôgen sint, wie reht min munt si, wie fúrig min herze ist, wie geringe min hende sint, wie snel min fůsse sint und volge mir. (p. 15)

> Vide mea sponsa: See how lovely are My eyes, how straight is My mouth, how fiery is My heart, how small are My hands, how quick are My feet, and follow Me.

By book 7, however, this sweetly erotic depiction of Christ has been replaced by evocations of the crucified Christ, such as the following:

> So sieh an dinen brútgômen, aller welte herren,
> Wie schône er gekleidet stůnt
> Mit pfellorinen cleidern, rot blůt,
> Swarz varwe, mit geiselen zersclagen,
> Zů der súle gebunden.
> Do enpfieng er dur dine liebin
> Manige scharpfen wunden.

> So sich vf, wie er an dem crúce stunt,
> Vfgerichtet hohe,
> Vor aller welte ôgen mit blůte beruñen.
> Die cleider sôllent wesen dines herzen wuñen,
> Sine keyserlichú ôgen mit trehnen vͬbervlossen,

> Dc leret dich die gotzmiñe,
> Wie der smiden hañere klopfeten und slůgen
> Dur sine hende und vôsse an dem crúze.

(p. 242)

Behold then your bridegroom, lords of the world,
How beautifully He stood clothed
With silken cloth, red blood,
Black color, scourged with lashes,
Bound to the pillar.
There He received for the sake of your love
Many sharp wounds.

Look up at how He stood on the cross
Lifted up high,
Dripping with blood before the eyes of the world.
The garments should be your hearts' bliss,
His imperial eyes overflowing with tears,

The love of God teaches you
How the smiths' hammers beat and drove
Through His hands and feet to the cross.

In spite of the fact that these two passages are quite different in emphasis, there is nevertheless a unifying theme: each is a specific manifestation of the soul's love for God. In the first passage love is evoked as erotic physical beauty; in the second as self-sacrifice, exemplified by the wounds, tears, and blood of Christ.

Milk

There is also found in *Das fliessende Licht* another liquid that, like blood, is of the earth but nevertheless possesses divine nourishment for the loving soul: the milk that flows from the breasts of the Virgin Mary. The similarity of Christ's blood and Mary's milk seems to be emphasized intentionally by Mechthild, because the two liquids are frequently juxtaposed in her work, thus implying an analogy between the two. In a description of heaven in book I Mechthild described how Mary and Christ stand at the left and right sides respectively of God. Christ stands with open wounds and Mary with exposed and flowing breasts:

> Do wart gesehen . . . wie der menschlich licham ist getempert und geformet in die edel lúhtnisse der sele vnser fröwen, und wie die lustlichen brúste vnverborgen sint vol der suessen milche, dc die tropfen vliessent dahin dem himelschen vatter ze eren und dem menschen ze liebe, also das der mensche vber alle creature wilkomen si . . . .
> Zů der vordern hant vnsers herren stat Jesus, vnser löser mit offenen wunden,
> Blutig, unverbunden,
> Ze úberwindende des vaters gerehtekeit,
> Die mangen súnder vil nahe leit,
> Wan diewile dc die súnde uf ertrich weret,
> So söllent Christi wunden offen sin,
> Blůtig ane sere.

(p. 29)

Then was seen . . . how the human body is tempered and formed in the noble likeness of the soul of our Lady and how her lovely breasts, exposed, are so full of the sweet milk that the drops flow down in honor of the heavenly Father and out of love for humanity, so that humanity is welcomed above all creatures . . . .
At the right hand of our Lord stood Jesus, our Redeemer, with open wounds,
Bloody, unbandaged,
To overcome the Father's righteousness
That hangs over many a sinner;
But, as long as sin endures on earth,
Christ's wounds shall be open,
Bleeding without pain.

This implicit analogy between the wounds and blood of Christ and the breasts and milk of Mary is made more explicit in a later passage. Christ describes the similarity of the two and simultaneously implies that, while both His blood and Mary's milk are of the earth, they both represent divine grace:

Min licham wc do menschlich tot,
Do min herzeblût
Mit der stralen der gotheit dur mine siten vlos.
Das blût kam von gnaden ze glicher wis alse die milch,
Die ich von miner megetlichen mûter søg.

(p. 201)

My body then was mortally dead
When My heart's blood
Along with the rays of the divine flowed through My side.
By grace the blood came in the same manner as the milk
That I sucked from My maiden mother.

Mechthild ascribed transcendent qualities to Mary's milk both because of Mary's significance as the prototypical loving soul and because of her participation in the ultimate paradox and miracle, the birth of God as a man. Mechthild was continually awed by the miracle of Christ and dwelled at great length on the paradoxes involved in His birth, life, and physical death. Because Christ was God-become-man, He like all men became subject to physical needs, to hunger and thirst. Simultaneously, however, because Christ was divine, Mechthild implied that His physical needs could be fulfilled only by the purest of physical substances. Mary is characterized by her immaculateness and Mechthild, therefore, implied that the milk that comes from her body is a transcendently pure physical substance. Her milk is in itself a paradox, because physicality normally implies inherent corruption. In a long description of the birth of Christ in book 1, Mechthild portrayed, by means of a series of paradoxes, a scene of physical interaction that is characterized, however, by sublime purity and spirituality:

Und dc kint wart hungerig und kalt.
Do mûste dú mûter iren sun stillen, . . .

Do neigte sich dú jungfröwe mit mûterlicher liebi
In megtlicher zuht
Ze irem gepingeten kinde
Und bot im ir kintliche brust.
    Hôret nu wunder:
Die lúhtende blûiunge ir schônen ögen
Und die geistliche schôni irs megtlichen antlitz
Und die vliessende sûssekeit irs reinen herzen
Und die wunenkliche spilunge ir edelen sele—
Dise vier ding zugen sich zesamene . . .

In ir megdtliche brust.
Do vlos dú sûsse milch harus von irme reinen herzen
Ane allen smerzen.
Do soug dc kint mônschliche . . . .

                                            (pp. 149–50)

And the child became hungry and cold.
Then the mother had to quiet her son, . . .

Then the virgin bent down with maternal love
And maidenly dignity
To her troubled child
And offered him her childlike breast.
    Now hear this wonder:
The glowing bloom of her beautiful eyes
And the spiritual beauty of her maidenly countenance
And the flowing sweetness of her pure heart
And the blissful swirling of her noble soul—
These four things came together . . .

In her maidenly breast.
Then the sweet milk flowed out from her pure heart
Without pain.
Then the child sucked humanly. . . .

Mary's milk is produced not by any normal physical process but rather by a miraculous combining of four nonphysical qualities ("Dies vier ding zugen sich zesaṁene . . . In ir megdtliche brust" ["These four things came together . . . in her maidenly breast"]). The milk, like Christ's blood, is of the earth but is not tainted by the earth and Mechthild thus implied that the ultimate origin of these liquids was divine ("Das blůt kam *von gnaden* ze glicher wis alse die milch" ["By grace the blood came in the same manner as the milk"]).

In an unmistakable analogy to the nourishing of Christ by Mary, Mechthild also broadened the significance of milk imagery in an extended metaphor describing the nourishing of all the children of God by the Mother Church:

> dc sich der himelsche vater erbarmete und gewan do zwene súne [priests and monks] in einer trahte aber bi vnser lieben můter, der heligen cristanheit, und si sögete selber dise zwene súne ja mit iren brústen, die also vol der sůssen milch sint, dc si si nie und öch niemer me mögent volle sugen us. Dise brúste . . . do vnser můter dú helige cristanheit mitte sögent allú gotteskint. (p. 155)

> the heavenly Father took mercy and gained then two sons in one birth through our dear mother, holy Christianity, and she herself suckled these two sons with her breasts that are so full of the sweet milk that they can never ever suck them dry. These breasts . . . with which our mother, holy Christianity, suckles all children of God.

In this passage milk represents not the maternal love of Mary for Christ but rather the love of God for all Christian souls. Milk is thus seen as another manifestation of the greater eternal liquid, the "miñevlůt" ("flood of love").

Because of the universality of the nourishment symbolism of Mary's breasts and milk, Mary was considered by Mechthild to be the mother not only of Christ but also of the Church, of souls, and curiously of all the prophets who had lived, physically, before her. Mary is in Mechthild's work a transcendent and universal mother figure whose total maternal qualities (love, care, tenderness, nourishment, and so forth) are all epitomized in the significance of the milk that flows eternally from her breasts.

> Do ich also mûter was maniges edeln kindes, do wurden mine brûste also vol der reinen vnbewollener milch der waren milten barmherzigkeit, das ich sôgete die propheten und die wissagen e deñe got geborn wart. Darnach in miner kintheit sôgete ich Jesum; fúrbas in miner jugent sôgete ich gotz brut die heligen cristanheit bi dem crûtze, das ich also dúrre und jemerlich wart, das das swert der vleischlicher pine Jesu sneit geistlich in min sele. Do stûnden offen beiden, sine wunden und ir brúste. Die wunden gussen, die brúste vlussen also, das lebendig wart die sele und gar gesunt. (p. 12)

When I was mother of many a noble child, my breasts became so full of the pure effortless milk of true compassion that I suckled the prophets and the wise men before God was born. Later in my childhood I suckled Jesus; still later I suckled God's bride, holy Christianity, at the cross so that I became dry and wretched and the sword of Jesus' physical pain cut spiritually into my soul. Then both stood open, His wounds and her breasts. The wounds poured, the breasts flowed so that the soul came to life and was well.

The soul of man had been dead ("sin liebú brut was tot, die edel sele" ["His dear bride was dead, the noble soul"] [p. 12]) between the time of the expulsion from the Garden and the birth of Christ. With the coming of Christ, however, the soul had been rejuvenated and returned to life by divine love. God can love the soul in many ways (father, brother, friend, confessor, doctor, and lover, as is related, for example, in book 7 [pp. 247–49]); Mary alone, however, can love the soul maternally. God is the eternal father, brother, friend, and lover of the soul; Mary is the eternal feminine ideal, the perpetual mother of the soul:

> Solte [die sele] do nach irem tode und ir geburt volleklich genesen, so mûste gottes mûter ir mûter und ir ame sin . . . .
> Vrowe, noch mûst du uns sôgen, wan dine brûste sind noch also vol, das du nút maht verdruken. Woltostu nit sôgen me, so tete dir die milch vil we. Wañ werlich ich han gesehen dine brúste also vol, das siben stralen gussen, alzemale us von einer brúste úber minen lip und úber min sele. (pp. 12–13)

If the soul is to recover completely after its death and its birth, then God's mother must be its mother and nurse. . . .
Lady, you must continue to suckle us for your breasts are still so full that you can not hold back the milk. If you would no longer suckle, the milk would cause you pain. For truly I have seen your breasts so full that seven streams poured at one time from one breast over my body and over my soul.

Just as God is forced by His nature to love the soul, so too is Mary forced by her nature, her own perpetual motherhood, to love the soul maternally and give eternal sustenance to the soul: "Woltostu nit sôgen me, so tete dir die milch vil we" ("If you would no longer suckle, the milk would cause you pain").

It should also be noted that because Mary serves as the ideal feminine being, the prototypical soul, and because she is characterized primarily by her breasts and milk, the suck-

ling of a baby is used as a metaphor for the love activity
between God and the soul. Mary was the mother of God
but the soul is His bride. Because of this dual relationship,
there is found in Mechthild's work an overlapping or intermingling of maternal and erotic forms of love. A mother's
nursing a baby represents in effect both maternal and erotic
love, combining emotional and physical pleasure. The
spiritualization of motherhood and the deemphasis of its
physical, erotic aspects are products of the postmedieval
era. Mechthild apparently believed that the erotic life of a
woman includes motherhood and that erotic as well as
maternal emotions flow quite naturally in both a woman-
man and a woman-child relationship.

This phenomenon is emphasized by the terminology that
Mechthild employed to describe the interaction both of
Mary and Christ and of the soul and God and is demonstrated by Mechthild's use of the words *küssen* ("to kiss")
and *sugen* ("to suck" or "to suckle"). The mother-child relationship is sometimes given erotic overtones by the word
küssen and, more frequently, the male-female love relationship of God and the soul is characterized by the word *sugen*.
An example of the first is found at the end of the passage
discussed above: "Eja, darnach søllen wir bekeñen und
sehen in unzellicher lust die milch und øch dieselbe brust,
die Jesus so dikke hat gekust" ("Ah, accordingly we should
recognize and regard with inexpressible pleasure the milk
and also this breast that Jesus so often kissed") (p. 13).

As the relationship of Christ and Mary is tinged with a
slight eroticism, so is the essentially erotic relationship of
Christ and soul colored by the soul's identification with the
motherliness of Mary. Thus one frequently finds the word
sugen used where *küssen* might have been thought more
appropriate or consistent. In book 1 Christ as the lamb "søg

ir [the soul's] herze mit sinem sůssen munde. Je me es sŏg, je me si es im gonde" ("sucked her heart with His sweet mouth. The more He sucked, the more she gave Him") (p. 33). Similarly in book 6 in a description of the *unio mystica:* "So begiñet si ze sugende, dc er miñesiech wirt ("Then she begins to suck so that he becomes sick with love") (p. 176), and in a description of the eternal union in heaven: "si wuneclicher gebruchent und tiefer sugent in die heligen drivaltekeit . . ." ("they enjoy more ecstatically and suck in more deeply the Holy Trinity . . . .") (p. 157).

Mechthild's use of the word *sugen* is, of course, directly related to the general occurrence of terms of eating and drinking as physical metaphors of the spiritual nourishing of the soul by God and of God by the soul. It is clear, too, that the significance of the milk imagery in Mechthild's work is related to her general employment of liquids to represent the nourishing love that flows between heaven and earth.

Wine

Dew, rain, blood, and milk are all manifestations of the eternal "miñevlůt." Similarly, wine was frequently used by Mechthild to represent divine love, apparently because of the identification of wine with the blood of Christ at the Last Supper and in the Eucharist. In the same passage in which Mechthild described the similarity of Christ's blood and Mary's milk (book 1, pp. 12–13), she also at one point referred to the liquid that flows from Christ's wounds not as blood but as wine:

Do er [Christ] den blanken roten *win* gos in iren [the soul's] munt, do si alsust vs den offen *wunden* geborn und lebendig wart, do was si kindisch und vil jung [italics added]. (p. 12)

When He poured the sparkling red *wine* into her mouth, she was born of the open *wounds* and brought to life, and she was childlike and very young.

This identification of wine and the blood of Christ is even more explicit in a passage from book 4 in which Christianity or the Church is personified as a beautiful maiden with a chalice in her hand filled with the blood of Christ:

Si treit in irer vordern hant einen kelch mit rotem wine, den trinket si alleine in vnzellicher wuñe, die engele versůchent sin niemer. Dc ist des ewigen sunes blůt . . . . (p. 96)

She bears in her right hand a chalice with red wine that she alone drinks in indescribable joy; the angels never taste it. That is the blood of the everlasting Son . . . .

Although the meaning of the wine imagery is directly derived from the meaning of eucharistic wine as a symbol of Christ's blood, this basic meaning is extended or generalized by Mechthild so that wine signifies a variety of things. Wine represents Christ's blood and Christ's suffering but also represents for Mechthild Christ Himself or the Holy Spirit or the love that flows from God to man. That wine can signify Christ or God is demonstrated by a description of the *unio mystica* in book 1: "So tůt er si in sin glůgendes herze alse sich der hohe fúrste und die kleine dirne alsust behalsent und vereinet sint als wasser und win" ("Then He puts her in His glowing heart as the high Prince and the little maid embrace and are united as water and wine") (p. 7). At this early point in her work Mechthild was less concerned with the suffering of Christ or the required suffering of the soul attempting to find God than she was with the joyously ecstatic condition of the soul in union with God. Her purpose in this early passage was to show the inherent similarity of the soul and God rather than to demonstrate the soul's need to make itself like God. Therefore she described God and the soul as wine and water, simultaneously demonstrating the possibility of an intermingling of the two and also their relative values. The soul as water is plentiful; God as wine is scarce and precious. The two are of similar liquidity, but one is of infinitely greater value than the other. In another passage it is not God or Christ who is represented as wine but rather the Holy Spirit: "der himelsche vatter da ist der seligen schenke und Jesus der kopf, der helig geist der luter win, und wie die ganze drivaltekeit ist der volle kopf, und miñe der gewaltige keller, —weis got, so neme ich gerne, das mich die miñe da ze huse bete" ("the heavenly Father is the blessed server there and Jesus the chalice and the Holy Spirit the pure wine, and the entire Trinity is the filled chalice and love the mighty cellar —God knows I would gladly partake so that love would bid me dwell there") (pp. 46–47). The Holy Spirit is the wine that flows to the soul out of the wine cellar that is divine love in general.

In other passages love is not the wine cellar but rather the wine itself; and this meaning is the most common significance of wine in Mechthild's work. In the following passage wine represents divine love or at least the soul's experiencing of divine love: "Ich wil ein wenig trinken den vngemengeten win" ("I want to drink a little of the undiluted wine") (p. 20). And in still another passage Mechthild expanded the original meaning of the wine imagery. The blood of Christ represents suffering, which is portrayed as red wine and contrasted with another manifestation of divine love, the white wine of comfort. Christ tells the soul that white wine is nobler but that the noblest soul will drink both wines, white and red, during its existence on earth:

Do hůp vnser herre zwene guldin kǒpffe in sinen henden,
die waren bede vol lebendiges wines. In der linggen hant
waz der rote win der pine, und in der vordren hant der
v́berhere trost. Do sprach vnser herre: Solich sint die
disen win trinkent, wand alleine ich bede schenke von
gotlicher liebi, so ist doch der wisse edeler in im selber
und aller edlest sint die, die beide trinkent wissen und
roten. (p. 35)

Then our Lord lifted in His hands two golden chalices
that were both full of living wine. In the left hand was
the red wine of pain and in the right hand enormous con-
solation. Then our Lord spoke: Blessed are those who
drink this wine for though I pour both from divine love
the white is nobler in itself and noblest of all are those
who drink both white and red.

That wine represents love is also implied in the numerous
passages such as the following one in which the soul is
compared to a container for God's love: "Was hilfet, das
man ein ital vas vil bindet, / Und das der win doch
usriñet?" ("What good does it do to bind an empty keg, /
If the wine still runs out?") (p. 44).

Although the specific meanings of wine change within
Mechthild's work, its general significance is almost always
a beneficial form of contact and interaction between God
and the soul. Wine is the liquid substance that signifies the
ultimate fulfillment of the soul's longing for God. The soul
seeks "den vngemengeten win" ("the undiluted wine") (p.
20) and can be truly satisfied by no other liquid. Therefore,
it is interesting to find that, in Mechthild's description of
the birth of Christ, Mary shows her utter humility by re-
fusing wine in favor of water:

Do vragete ich Marien wo Joseph were.
Do sprach si, er ist in die stat gangen

Vnd köfet vns kleine vische und gemeines brot,
Und wasser trunken si öch.
Do sprach ich: Eya vröwe,
Du soltest essen das allerschöneste brot,
Und trinken den alleredelosten win.
Nein, sprach si, das ist richer lúte spise,
Der haben wir nit in disem armen libe.

(p. 150)

Then I asked Mary where Joseph was.
Then she spoke, "He has gone into the city
And is buying for us little fish and common bread."
And water they also drank.
Then I spoke, "Ah, Lady,
You should eat the finest bread
And drink the noblest wine."
"No," she said, "that is rich people's food
That we do not have in this poor life."

The most interesting use of the wine imagery is found in Mechthild's descriptions of the *unio mystica* as an intoxication of the soul. One of the primary sources for this concept is again the Song of Songs and Mechthild acknowledged this influence in a passage in book 3:

Salomones wort lúhtend und sine werk nit, wan er selber vervinstert ist, in dem bůche canticis, da dú brut so trunken kuene vunden ist und der brútegöme so rehte nötlich ir zů sprichet: du bist alles schöne, min frúndine und kein flekke ist an dir. (p. 81)

Solomon's words illuminate (though not his works for he himself is darkened) in the book *Canticles:* "There the bride is found so drunkenly bold and the bridegroom speaks to her so urgently: 'You are all beautiful, my friend, and no stain is on you!'"

In addition to this influence, Lüers mentions the possibility that Mechthild was continuing the general mystical tradition of describing the soul's consumption of magic liquids or elixirs that intoxicate the soul.[1] In any event, in Mechthild's descriptions of the mystical union the soul and Christ become intoxicated by each other: "Die brut ist trunken worden von der angesihte des edeln antlútes" ("The bride became drunk by the sight of the noble countenance") (p. 11), or "Dc er also miñenvúrig trunken was" ("So that He was drunk as with love's fire") (p. 246). This image is utilized to the fullest in an extended passage in book 3 in which Mechthild described the soul as a winedrinker who comes to the tavern of divine love where God is the innkeeper. The soul has an insatiable desire for wine, but the wine can be purchased only with the coin of earthly suffering:

> Ich was vrõliche wan trunken in der miñe, darumbe sprach ich zartlich von siñen. Sweñe ich aber werde vbertrunken, so mag ich mines liebes nit gedenken, wan dú miñe gebútet mir, dc si wil dc mũs sin, ...

> Wilt du [sele] mit mir [miñe] in die winzelle gan,
> So mũstu grosse kosten han.
> Hastu tausend marche wert.
> Dc hastu (in) einer stunde verzert.

> Wilt du den win ungemenget trinken, so verzerest du jemer me als du hast, so mag dir der wirt nit volle schenken. So wirstu arm und nakent und von allen den versmehet, die lieber sich frõwent in dem pfũle, denne si iren schaz in der hohen winzelle vertũn.

> Du mũst õch das liden,
> Das dich dieiene niden,
> Die mit dir in die winzelle gant.
> O wie sere si dich ettesweñe versmahent,
> Wan si so grosse koste nit getõrrent bestan.
> Si wellent das wasser ze dem wine gemenget han.

Liebe vrŏ brut, in der tauerne wil ich gerne
Verzeren alles das ich han . . . .

Darumbe der mich piniget und versmehet, der schenket
mir des wirtes win, den er selbe getrunken hat.

Von dem wine werde ich also trunken,
Dc ich allen creaturen werlich wirde als vndertan, . . .

(pp. 63–64)

I was joyously drunk from love; therefore I spoke
tenderly of the senses. But when I become overly drunk
then I can not think of my love, for love bids me that
what it wants must be, ...

"If you (soul) want to go with me (love) to the wine cellar,
Then you must have much money.
If you have a thousand marks
You will have spent it in an hour.

If you want to drink the wine undiluted, then you will
always spend more than you have and then the host can
not fill your glass. Then you will become poor and naked
and despised by all those who would rather frolic in the
mud than squander their treasure in the high wine cellar.

You must also endure
That those will envy you
Who go with you to the wine cellar.
O how much they will sometimes revile you,
For they dare not pay such great costs.
They want to have water mixed into the wine."
"Dear Lady Bride, in the tavern I will gladly
Spend all that I have . . . .

Therefore whoever torments and reviles me pours for me
the host's wine that He drank Himself.

From this wine I become so drunk
That I truly become subject to all creatures, ..."

Despite some curious ideas, this passage is notable because Mechthild succeeded in making her extended metaphor fit so perfectly into her total framework of religious belief. Wine, as has been seen, is a traditional metaphor, directly for the blood of Christ and indirectly for the love of God. Intoxication is an appropriate description of the state of the soul within the *unio mystica,* portraying as it does the bliss and transcendent elation of a soul freed from earthly, physical restraints. The analogy is extended to include even the concept of the imitation of the sufferings of Christ as a means to heavenly bliss; the wine is purchased with money that the soul earns by its endurance of earthly degradation and misery. This passage is also interesting because of the virtue found in the overindulgence of the soul, in spite of the fact that physical immoderation is a despised vice. Intoxication by earthly things is evil; intoxication in God is good. On earth moderation in food and drink must be maintained because overindulgence leads the soul away from God. Intoxication in God, however, is encouraged because it leads the soul away from the earth and gives the soul a total involvement in God. Moderation is a virtue only of the soul on earth.

Honey, Tears and Gall

Wine, along with blood, milk, and water from heaven, is one of the most prevalent examples of Mechthild's reliance on liquid images to symbolize the love of God for man and the interaction of God and man. In addition to these four images, there are a number of other liquids that, although appearing less frequently, nevertheless have a similar significance in Mechthild's work: honey, tears, and gall.

Honey, rather than representing divine love itself (as do the four primary liquids), seems to signify wisdom, the soul's

knowledge of God or of His truths. In the allegory of the
spiritual animal "alles nútze" in book 4 the exact significance
of the honey that the animal sucks from its own tail is not
specifically identified: "Die tier isset nit mere, es hat einen
grossen zagel, der ist vol honiges, den suget es alle tage . . .
der lip wirt gespiset von des süssen honiges trank" ("The
animal no longer eats; it has a large tail filled with honey
that it sucks every day . . . the body is nourished by the
sweet honey drink") (p. 112). It is clear, however, that the
honey does not represent God's love ("Die guldine grañe,
das ist die edel gotzmiñe" ["The golden whiskers are the
noble love of God"] [p. 112]). In a passage in book 7 honey
is again mentioned by Mechthild but again with no precise
significance attributed to it except that it is some type of
gift from God to the soul:

> Du solt mir honges trank behalten,
> Der liget in maniger valden;
> Ich wil în vf scliessen;
> Des sol noch maniger geniessen.

(p. 257)

> You shall receive from Me a honey drink
> That lies in many a fold;
> I will open it up;
> Still others may enjoy it.

At other times honey seems to be employed as a symbol of
divine truth. In one passage Mechthild implied this meaning
and described herself as a bee struggling with the impossibility of carrying away all the honey at one time:

Den kôren und dem hiñele ist von gotte manig wúrdekeit
   gegeben,
Do mag ich von jegelichem ein wôrtelin sagen.

Dc ist nit me deñe also vil,
Als ein bini honges mag
Vs einem vollen stok an sinem fûsse getragen.

(p. 60)

Much worthiness is given by God to the choirs and to heaven
Of which I can say only a little word.
That is no more
Than the honey that a bee can
Carry on its foot out of a full hive.

This interpretation of the significance of honey imagery is reinforced by the association of honey with the apostles in book 4. Here a beautiful young woman, the personification of Christianity, is described as having golden coins in her mouth, lips made of roses, nostrils stuffed with violets, and honey dripping from her tongue: "Ir trúfet honig vs ir zungen, dc die snellen binen, die heiligen aposteln, vs den sûssesten veltblûmen hant gesogen" ("From her tongue drips honey that the quick bees, the holy apostles, have sucked from the sweetest flowers of the field") (p. 97).

In the above passage Mechthild again demonstrated the influence of the Song of Songs upon her imagery: "Thy lips, my spouse, are as a dropping honeycomb, honey and milk are under thy tongue" (Song of Songs 4:11). Although Mechthild used imagery similar to that of the Song of Songs, her meaning bears a strong resemblance to a more common Biblical significance of honey. As found in Ecclesiasticus and Proverbs, for example, honey is associated with wisdom: "For my [Wisdom's] spirit is sweet above honey, and my inheritance above honey and the honeycomb" (Ecclesiasticus 24:27).

While honey seems to represent wisdom or knowledge of the divine, tears signify self-knowledge, that is, the soul's knowledge or awareness of its own sins and weaknesses. Because repentance and self-knowledge prepare the soul for salvation, tears, like water and blood, possess the ability to purify and rejuvenate the soul. The purification that tears can bestow is, moreover, not limited to one's own soul but rather can be gained for the souls of other men. In a passage in book 2, Mechthild described indulgences gained for souls in purgatory by the tears of men on earth. Mechthild envisioned suffering souls in purgatory and asked God how they can be helped. God tells her to bathe them in a basin filled with the tears of love—an apparent parallel to the baptismal font:

> Do neigete got vnmassen sere nider sine edelkeit und sprach ein wort, das uns súndigen sere ze troste stat: Du solt si baden in den miñe trehnen, die da nu vliessent usser den ogen dines lichamen. Do wart da gesehen ein sinwel grosse. Da hûben si sich mit einem swunge zemale in, und badoten in der miñe klar als die suñe. Do enphieng des menschen geist unzelliche wuñe . . . . (pp. 35–36)

> Then God bent down His nobility immeasurably low and spoke a word that is of great solace to us sinners: You shall bathe them in the tears of love that now flow from the eyes of your body. Then was seen a great basin. With a leap they jumped in at once and bathed in love clear as the sun. Then the human spirit received inexpressible bliss . . . .

The relation of tears to blood as a purifier is also implied by Mechthild in an allegory of the Church as an eternal, gigantic crown: "Die crone ist gezúget . . . mit menschlichen trehenen, sweis unde blût" ("The crown is made . . . with human tears, sweat, and blood") (p. 218).

Like blood, tears represent a paradoxical aspect of salvation: the purchasing of spiritual redemption by earthly pain and suffering. Although tears can represent sympathy and

charitable love, they more usually represent the soul's regret
for its own errors and thus offer a means to redemption:
"vil trehenen mit rúwigem herze us reinen ŏgen gebe, das
solte min bŭsse sin und wesen" ("with a repentant heart shed
many tears from pure eyes, that shall be my penance") (p.
79). Mechthild believed, however, that tears possess redemp-
tive power only if they arise from a truly repentant soul.
Only tears evoked by regret are sanctified:

> Vrŏw ware rúwe, koment har zŭ mir
> Und bringent mir helige trehene,
> Die machen mich súnde ane.

(p. 262)

> Lady true repentance, come here to me
> And bring me holy tears
> That take away my sins.

Mechthild used the adjective *ware* because regret can be
feigned. Only genuine regret can produce "helige" tears.
Other tears, "súndige trehne," can be summoned up by an
insincere soul or by anger, but these tears have no spiritual
merit:

> Aber owe! die súndige trehne rúwent mich, die man
> weinot in homŭtigem zorne. Da wirt die sele also vinster
> von, dc der mensche diewile keiner gŭter dinge rehte kan
> gebruchen.
> Die rúwige trehne sint also helig; mŏhte ein grosser
> súnder einen rúwigen trehnen vmb alle sine súnde weinen,
> er keme niemer zŭ der ewigen helle, blibe er also. (p. 224)

> But alas! I regret the sinful tears that are wept in
> proud anger. From these the soul becomes so dark that
> for a time the human being can do nothing good.
> Repentant tears are thus holy: were a great sinner to
> shed one repentant tear for all his sins, he would never go
> to everlasting hell if he stayed that way.

Thus tears, because they are a visible sign of sincere spiritual regret, possess the power of purifying and redeeming the soul. Tears arise because of sin; and, therefore, it can be seen that even evil can paradoxically serve as a force of ultimate good if the erring soul can be made to see God's truth.

Equally paradoxical is the function that Mechthild ascribed to the liquid gall ("galle"). This liquid is the earthly antithesis of the heavenly wine. Gall represents the earthly bitterness and suffering that the soul is forced to endure before wine is granted by God. The thirst of the soul is for the pure, sweet wine of God but, on earth, the soul is usually given only gall to drink.

The opposition of gall and wine in Mechthild's work is a divergence from the more traditional opposition of gall and honey. The traditional antithesis is, to be sure, also found in *Das fliessende Licht,* as it is in the passage: "dc du . . . die gallen miner bitterkeit ze honig wellist machen in dem gŏme miner sele" ("that you will turn the gall of my bitterness to honey in the palate of my soul") (p. 169). Equally often, however, the gall of suffering is opposed to the wine of bliss, and this image, too, seems to have a partial basis in the circumstances of the Crucifixion:

And they came to the place called Golgotha, that is, the Place of the Skull. And they gave him wine to drink mixed with gall. (Matthew 27:33–34)

Similarly, in a description of the crucifixion of the soul on earth in imitation of the Passion of Christ, Mechthild wrote:

Si dúrstet ŏch vil sere an dem crúze der miñe, wan si trunke vil gerne den luteren win von allen gotzkinden.

> So koment si al mit alle
> Und schenkent ir die galle.
>
> (p. 72)

She also thirsts greatly on the cross of love for she would like to drink the pure wine from all God's children.
> Then they come all together
> And offer gall to her.

Despite the suffering involved, gall is a blessing for the soul, because the soul's endurance of its bitterness eventually brings to the soul the wine of God:

> Nu ich wil noch hie gerne gallen trinken. Eya lieber Jesu, nu lone es inen allen liplich, die mir hie schenkent bitterkeit, wan si machent mich gnadenrich. Mir kam ein kopf mit gallen, der was also kreftig, das er min lip und sele al durgieng. Do bat ich sunderlich got fúr minen schenken, das er im wólte schenken den himelschen win. Werlich das tet er und sprach: Du juncfrowe, gehabe dich wol. Die gróssi mines wunders sol v́ber dich gan, ... Ich bin des gewiss, unde als mir vntzhar ist beschehen, das ich noch manigen kopf mit gallen vs sol trinken. (p. 47)

> Here I will gladly drink gall. Ah dear Jesus, now lovingly reward all those who gave me bitterness for they make me rich in grace. A chalice of gall came to me that was so strong that it went through my body and soul. Then I asked God especially for my cup that He would fill it with the heavenly wine. Truly He did that and spoke: "Maiden, be cheerful. The greatness of My miracle shall pass over you, ..." I am certain that, just as has happened to me up to now, I will still have many a chalice of gall to drink.

Thus nearly all the liquids in Mechthild's work, even tears and gall, function ultimately as beneficial in some way to the spiritual life of humanity. They purify, rejuvenate, sanctify, nourish, or (in the case of gall) prepare the soul.

There are only two liquids that totally lack beneficial qualities : the evil "saf," found in the apple that Adam and Eve
ate in the Garden, and menstrual blood :

> dc súndliche menschliche saf, das adam vs dem ôpfel
> beis, dc noch natúrlich allú unsre lider durgat, und darzů
> dc verflůchte blůt, dc Even und allen wiben von dem
> ôppfel entstůnt, ... Adam behielt dc saf an ime und
> danach alle man. Eva und allú wip behielten dis vil
> schemlich blůt. (pp. 137–38)

> the sinful human sap that Adam bit from the apple that
> still naturally runs through all our limbs, and also the
> cursed blood that came to Eve and all women from the
> apple, ... Adam kept the sap in him and afterwards in
> all men. Eve and all women kept this very shameful
> blood.

The sap and blood of this passage are obviously related to
the concept of original sin, but Mechthild's use of the image
of the Eden apple is interesting because of its analogy with
the image of Christ as an apple growing from the tree of
the Trinity. The dual significance of the apple image under-
lines Mechthild's concept of appearance and truth. By pre-
senting parallel images, the apple of Christ and the Eden
apple, she emphasized the importance of free will; the individual must discern between apparent and true beauty or
goodness.

The significance of sea water and of the sap of the Eden
apple, mentioned only once, is antithetical to the general
significance of liquid imagery in Mechthild's work. All other
liquids, all manifestations of the transitional element water
in *Das fliessende Licht* signify the eternal love between God
and the soul and the soul's transition from the corruption
of earth to the purity of God.

Note to Chapter 6

1. Lüers, p. 259.

7

Conclusion

Mechthild von Magdeburg was indebted, in both a theological and literary sense, to traditional literature and ideas, as Grete Lüers has persuasively demonstrated. Mechthild was of course aware of tradition and precedent, of ancient and early medieval thought, but she shaped these influences to make them harmonize with her mystical theology. The essence of mysticism, particularly intuitive mysticism, is highly individualized; Mechthild, therefore, employed traditional ideas and motifs to express her own idiosyncratic form of Christian mysticism. In addition, however, she drew upon contemporary knowledge and experience as a source for the imagery of *Das fliessende Licht*.

As a work of intuitive mysticism, Mechthild's work stands, in certain respects, outside the mainstream of medieval religious literature. Relative to many other medieval mystical writers, Mechthild was not well educated, as she admitted. Her work was written in the vernacular rather than Latin and bears only a limited resemblance to such theoretical works as those of Bernard of Clairvaux or Meister Eckhart, for example. Mechthild's literary intent was visionary description rather than theological speculation. Thus her themes are subject as much to her own fantasy as to medieval Catholic orthodoxy, as is evidenced by the ecclesiastic censure that Mechthild mentioned at various times in her work. Similarly the style and form of her work were subject at the last only to her own taste. *Das fliessende Licht* shows spontaneity of production; and only traces of sophisticated medieval rhetoric and poetic modes, rather than a conscious adherence to such contrived stylistic devices, are evident in Mechthild's work. Because of the lack of conscious form and style, because of the relative naivete of her work, one is justified in seeking at least a partial basis for Mechthild's imagery in the elements of everyday life of a thirteenth-century Dominican Beguine.

Because of the circumstances of Mechthild's life as a Christian and a Beguine, she was imbued with both the ideas of the medieval Church and with the Church's modes of expressing these ideas. Her work reflects, of course, the themes and imagery of the Bible (particularly of the Gospels) and of ecclesiastical commentaries on the Bible. Above and beyond this, however, there are discernible patterns of imagery that owe as much to the popular, secular thought of the Middle Ages as they do to the writings and dogma of the Church. In addition to the obvious influence of traditional Christian imagery, Lüers has pointed out the abundance of similes and metaphors drawn from medieval courtly life.[1] Thus, Mechthild frequently depicted God and Christ as emperor and prince of heaven (for example, p. 119, 212, or 242). She described the mystical union as the "hovereise der sele" ("the soul's journey to court"):

Swene die arme sele kumet ze hove, so ist si wise und wolgezogen; so siht si iren got vrolichen an. (p. 7)

When the poor soul comes to the court, she is wise and well-mannered; thus she regards her God with joy.

She represented the soul itself as a knight in a tournament; as the knight must serve his lord, so must the soul serve God:

> Do sprach vnser herre: . . . Behagete dir, dc du ein ritter were mit vollen waffenen und von edeler kunst unde mit warer mankraft und mit geringen henden, ... (p. 80)

> Then our Lord spoke: . . . Would it suit you if you were a knight with full armor and of noble art and with true manhood and with small hands, . . . ?

There is also found in Mechthild's work what Lüers called the influence "des täglichen Lebens, des Bürgertums, des Naturgefühls usw." [2] For example, God is represented as a physician (p. 248) or as a loving mother who protects her child, the soul, "Als ein mûter ir liebes kint / Vs der eschen in ir schosse hat genoṁen" ("As a mother has taken her dear child / Out of the ashes into her lap") (p. 117), or

> Hievon wart min sele also snell zů gotte . . . und bewant sich rehte in die heilige drivaltekeit, als ein kint sich bewindet in den mantel siner mûter und leit sich rehte an ir brust. (p. 183)

> At this my soul was swiftly with God . . . and wrapped itself in the holy Trinity as a child wraps itself in its mother's coat and lies down at her breast.

Similarly the influence of popular medieval scientific theory can also be perceived in Mechthild's work.

The images of courtly life and the representations of

God as a physician or a protective parent do not contradict the fundamentally orthodox concept of the divine that underlies Mechthild's thought but rather serve to reinforce the idea of God's spiritual healing and protection. These images add a new dimension to dogma and indicate an integration of the secular and the divine. Similarly, a consideration of Mechthild's imagery within the framework of medieval scientific thought in no way neglects or contradicts the essentially religious orientation of this imagery but rather reinforces it. The intent is to demonstrate not a secularization of the religious by Mechthild but rather the universal applicability of her religious beliefs. In Mechthild's work the imagery of the court, of everyday life, and of science serves not as a denial of religious truth but rather acts as a reflection of the divine, a "spiegel der gotheit" (p. 58).

There exist in Mechthild's work consistent and coherent patterns of imagery based on a combination of Biblical imagery and of the Hellenic elemental and cosmological system of four primary elements. Each of the four elements and their respective cosmological spheres have definite meanings.In particular, it is clear that water and liquids had for Mechthild a definite and consistent significance.

Mechthild's concern within *Das fliessende Licht* was a dual one. She, like most mystical poets, wanted first of all to explore the depths of her own religious consciousness and second to convey the totality of her mystical experience to her readers. Mechthild's work was intended to be, at least to some extent, didactic. She attempted to find images to visualize her ecstatic experiences and her beliefs. She therefore drew upon the natural world and the popular scientific theories of the construction of that world to illustrate her spiritual attitudes. Lynn Thorndike writes in his study of Hildegard von Bingen that she held the view, common among medieval Christian writers, that one purpose of the natural world about us is to illustrate the spiritual world and life to come, and that invisible and eternal truths may be manifested in visible and temporal objects.[3]

According to this view, which is evident also in Mechthild's work, the natural world is God's creation and thus reflects God's truths. The poet does not arbitrarily invent his images; rather they are inherent in man's environment, a part of God's creation. Thus, science or a knowledge of the natural world can supply intrinsic images of eternal truths.

As Mechthild's contemporary Thomas Aquinas synthesized Hellenic philosophy and Christian theology, so did Mechthild indicate a synthesis of Hellenic science and traditional Christian symbolism. Combining the Hellenic idea of water as one of the four primary elements with the Biblical symbolism of water as spirituality, Mechthild's work demonstrates a consistent imaginal pattern of water and liquids, representing the loving interaction of God and the soul.

While accepting much of the Hellenic elemental and cosmological systems without alteration, Mechthild at times redirected the emphasis of Hellenic thought by applying it to her own religious beliefs. For example, Aristotle had differentiated between the elements according to their relative densities or "lightness" and "heaviness." Mechthild, on the other hand, apparently considered as more important the motion or stasis that density effects. A theory of the motion of the elements is, to be sure, found in Aristotle's work and in fact serves as the foundation for his hypothesis of a fifth element. For Aristotle, however, motion was a secondary characteristic of density. Because of the relative densities of the elements, motion occurs with each element attempting to find its natural location in the universe. Fire, which is "light," naturally collects at the extremities of the universe while earth, being "heavy," gravitates to the center:

> As the elements have by nature the tendency to move in one particular direction, either to the center or away from it, so they also have their natural places in the Cosmos.[4]

In Mechthild's work the motion, or lack of motion, of the elements is more significant than density, because of the identification of motion with true spiritual life.

A fusion of the scientific idea of elemental motion with the religious idea of true and eternal existence is seen in the relative values assigned to the elements in Mechthild's work. Flesh is solid, heavy, tangible, and therefore identifiable as earth. Because of the identification of flesh with evil in the Christian tradition, earth, too, would be regarded as evil.[5] This religious concept is then reinforced by Hellenic scientific ideas that characterize the elements as representative of various stages of being and not-being, and equate earth with not-being:

> it is indeed necessary to distinguish among the elements—these prime elements—between some which have being and others which have not-being . . . . The common run of people will be inclined to regard air as not-being because it is not visible and to treat earth as being. For them it would be sufficient that what changes into air seems to pass away into nothing. A more philosophical approach would be to consider fire and air as real because they have a higher degree of form . . . ; under this point of view earth would be not-being.[6]

What Solmsen calls the "more philosophical approach" is also evident in Mechthild's imagery. Mechthild distinguishes between the approaches to being and not-being in her description of foolish souls who grasp apparent being that in truth is not-being and thereby lose all possibility of gaining true being, as in her metaphor of the fish lured by the bait of the "world's poison" (p. 242).

Related to this conception of true being, moreover, is the Hellenic view of the construction of the elements and their subsequent mobility. Motion is in Mechthild's work the ultimate sign of true being or true life, the life of the spirit, and in the Platonic and Neoplatonic systems earth is the least mobile of the elements:

> Constructing them [the elements] as he [Plato] does out of regular solid bodies, he points out that the element which is built up of pyramids, fire, has the greatest mobility whereas earth, which consists of cubes, is least mobile.[7]

Thus, according to Mechthild's view of human existence, of the flesh and the spirit, it can be seen that flesh and earth equal weight, immobility, and death. The soul, on the other hand, is invisible and, therefore, of a higher form than the body. It is the nature of all elements to move toward their natural spheres; similarly it is natural for the soul to move away from the body and toward God. The task of the soul is to achieve a transition from the sphere of earth to and beyond the sphere of fire, to achieve a transformation from heaviness, immobility, and not-being to lightness, motion, and being or eternal life. Water, the transitional element, thus represents the transition of the soul from earth toward God. In Mechthild's view this transition is achieved actually by divine love flowing between heaven and earth and metaphorically by water flowing between the ethereal and terrestrial spheres.

For Mechthild motion was all important because of its implications of freedom and joy for the soul. Motion as the natural companion of freedom and joy is a common poetic motif and is also found in a poem by Heinrich von Morungen:

> In sô hôe swebender wunne
> sô gestuont mîn herze an fröiden nie.
> ich var alse ich fliegen kunne
> mit gedanken iemer umbe sie,
> sît daz mich ir trôst enpfie,
> der mir durch die sêle mîn
> mitten in das herze gie.

> Swaz ich wunneclîches schouwe,
> daz spil gegen der wunne die ich hân.
> luft und erde, walt und ouwe,
> suln die zît der fröide mîn enpfân:
> mir ist komen ein hügender wân
> unde ein wunneclîcher trôst,
> des mîn muot sol hôe stân.[8]

> In such high and floating bliss
> My heart has never stood before.
> I walk as if I could fly
> With thoughts always of her,
> Since to me has been given her solace
> That went through my soul
> Straight into my heart.

> Let whatever blissful things I see
> Compete with the bliss I have.
> Let air and earth, forest and field,
> Share this period of my happiness.
> To me have come a joyous faith
> And a blissful solace;
> For all of this my spirit shall stand high.

The similarity in language and idea is unmistakable in both this poem and Mechthild's portrayal of souls in heaven:

> Die seligen die nu in dem himel swebent und da so wuneklichen lebent, die sint alle beuangen mit einem liehte, und sint durchflossen mit einer miñe und sint vereinet mit einem willen, ... (p. 59)

> The blessed who now float in heaven and live so blissfully there are all illuminated by one light and are penetrated by one love and are united by one will, ...

The point here is not to demonstrate any conscious influence on Mechthild's work by secular poetry but rather to indicate the general inclination of medieval and probably of most poets to associate motion ("sweben") with the joy ("wunne") that results from love, whether the love experience is secular or mystical. Each grants to the lover a transcendence of physical, earthly restraint and stagnation that is the normal condition of the spirit or soul.

In *Das fliessende Licht,* total freedom, joy, and motion are characteristic of the soul only after its transformation and transition from earth to heaven, from the realm of flesh to the realm of spirit. Freedom, joy, motion, and the true, eternal life of the soul are found only within the union with the divine and represent the fulfillment of the soul's striving. The soul must constantly strive to recapture this fulfillment, because it can be attained only infrequently and temporarily during the soul's existence on earth. Ecstatic union is a condition that must be pursued by both God and the soul, and in Mechthild's work this pursuit is represented by the imagery of water and liquids. Neither God nor the soul proceeds directly from heaven or earth to its polar opposite, its antithetical sphere. Each approaches the other through a transitional realm that combines tangibility and intangibility, visibility and invisibility, corporealty and spirituality, motionlessness and motion. Total motion is "sweben," which surpasses the mere flowing or "vliessen" of water. Water is nevertheless the intermediate state between earthly stasis and ethereal motion. Water and liquids symbolize the transformation effected by love that releases the soul from earth and carries it to the joy and freedom of purely spiritual existence with God. Love flows from the Trinity and streams in a perpetual flood between God and the soul of man; love purifies, nourishes, and transports the soul to eternal, blissful union with the divine:

dc ist die spilende miñevlůt, die von got heimlich in dú sele vlússet und si wider mit siner kraft nach îr maht. Was zwischent în beiden deñe wuñen si, dc weis niemen von den andern wc si wirken vnderen ander, wan ein jegliches vindet sinen teil; was er hie hat vsgeleit, dc wirt im dŏrt alles widergeben.

    Dis ist die hiñelsche gotz miñe,
    Die hie vil kleinliche begiñet
    Und dŏrt niemer ende gewiñet.

(p. 199)

that is the swirling flood of love that secretly flows from God into the soul and the soul flows back with His strength to the best of her ability. What, other than bliss, may be between the two, what effect they have on one another, no one else knows; but each one finds his part. Whatever one has given here will all be returned there.

    This is the heavenly love of God
    That has a small beginning here,
    And there never comes to an end.

Notes to Chapter 7

1. Lüers, pp. 55–80.
2. Ibid., p. 80; "of daily life, of the bourgeoisie, of the feeling for nature et cetera."
3. Lynn Thorndike, "Hildegard von Bingen," *A History of Magic and Experimental Science, During the First Thirteen Centuries of our Era,* Vol. 2 (New York: The Macmillan Company, 1923), p. 137.
4. Friedrich Solmsen, *Aristotle's System of the Physical World: A Comparison with his Predecessors* (Ithaca, N.Y.: Cornell University Press, 1960), p. 266.
5. A similar identification of the soul with goodness and of the body with evil is found also in the works of Plotinus. *See,* for example, "The Descent of the Soul" in: *The Essential Plotinus,* ed. and trans. Elmer O'Brien (New York: Mentor Books and The New American Library, 1964), pp. 59–71.
6. Solmsen, pp. 332–33.
7. Solmsen, p. 267.
8. *Des Minnesangs Frühling,* 34th., ed. Carl von Kraus (Stuttgart: S. Hirzel Verlag, 1967), pp. 162–63.

Bibliography

Ancelet-Hustache, Jeanne. *Mechtilde de Magdebourg (1207–1282), étude de psychologie religieuse.* Paris: Librairie Ancienne Honoré Champion, 1926.

Auerbach, Erich. *Literatursprache und Publikum in der lateinischen Spätantike und im Mittelalter.* Bern: Francke Verlag, 1958.

————. *Mimesis; dargestellte Wirklichkeit in der abendländischen Literatur.* Bern: Francke Verlag, 1946.

Bachelard, Gaston *L'eau et les Rêves. Essai sur l'imagination de la matière.* Paris: Librarie José Corti, 1942.

————. *The Psychoanalysis of Fire.* Translated by Alan C. M. Ross. Boston: The Beacon Press, 1964.

Bäuml, Franz H. *Medieval Civilization in Germany, 800–1273.* New York: Frederick A. Praeger, Inc., 1969.

Baldwin, Charles Sears. *Medieval Rhetoric and Poetic (to 1400). Interpreted from Representative Works.* Reprint. Gloucester, Mass.: Peter Smith, 1959.

Bernhart, Joseph *Die philosophische Mystik des Mittelalters von ihren antiken Ursprüngen bis zur Renaissance.* Vol. 14 of *Geschichte der Philosophie in Einzeldarstellungen: Abt. 3. Die christliche Philosophie.* Munich: Verlag Ernst Reinhardt, 1922.

Berthold, Luise. "Beobachtungen zur deutschen Mystik." *Germanisch-Romanische Monatsschrift,* 19 (1931): 461–62.

Boor, Helmut de, and Newald, Richard. *Die deutsche Literatur im späten Mittelalter: Zerfall und Neubeginn.* Vol. 3 of *Geschichte der deutschen Literatur von den Anfängen bis zur Gegenwart.* Munich: C. H. Beck, 1962.

Buchberger, Michael, ed. *Lexikon für Theologie und Kirche.* Freiburg i. Br.: Herder & Co., 1934.

Campbell, Joseph, *The Hero with a Thousand Faces.* 2d ed. Princeton, N. J.: Princeton University Press, 1968.

Cirlot, J. E. *A Dictionary of Symbols.* New York: Philosophical Library, 1962.

Clark, James M. *The Great German Mystics: Eckhart, Tauler and Suso.* Oxford: Basil Blackwell, 1949.

Crombie, Alistair Cameron. *Medieval and Early Modern Science.* 2d ed. Cambridge, Mass.: Harvard University Press, 1967.

Curtius, Ernst Robert. *Europäische Literatur und Lateinisches Mittelalter.* 6th ed. Bern: A. Francke Verlag, 1967.

Dillistone, Frederick William. *Christianity and Symbolism.* Philadelphia: The Westminster Press, 1955.

Donaldson, E. Talbot; Kaske, R. E.; and Donahue, Charles. "Patristic Exegesis in the Criticism of Medieval Literature: The Opposition, the Defense, and Summation." In *"Critical Approaches to Medieval Literature.* Edited with a Foreword by Dorothy Bethurum. New York: Columbia University Press, 1960.

Eliade, Mircea. *Images and Symbols.* Translated by Philip Mairet. New York: Sheed & Ward, 1961.

Gall Morel, P., ed. *Offenbarungen der Schwester Mechthild von Magdeburg oder Das fliessende Licht der Gottheit.* Reprint. Darmstadt: Wissenschaftliche Buchgesellschaft, 1963.

Gilson, Etienne. *The Mystical Theology of Saint Bernard.* Translated by A. H. C. Downes. London and New York: Sheed & Ward, 1940.

Grabmann, Martin. "Die deutsche Frauenmystik des Mittelalters. Ein Überblick." In *Mittelalterliches Geistesleben; Abhandlungen zur Geschichte der Scholastik und Mystik.* Vol. 1. Munich: M. Hueber Verlag, 1926.

Grundmann, Herbert. "Die geschichtlichen Grundlagen der deutschen Mystik." *Deutsche Vierteljahrsschrift für Literaturwissenschaft und Geistesgeschichte* 12 (1934): 400–29.

――――. *Religiöse Bewegungen im Mittelalter. Untersuchungen über die geschichtlichen Zusammenhänge zwischen der Ketzerei, den Bettelorden und der religiösen Frauenbewegung im 12. und 13. Jahrhundert und über die geschichtlichen Grundlagen der deutschen Mystik.* Reprint. Hildesheim: Georg Olms Verlagsbuchhandlung, 1961.

――――. "Zur Geschichte der Beginen im 13 Jahrhundert." *Archiv für Kulturgeschichte* 21 (1931): 296–320.

Harper, Ralph. *Human Love—Existential and Mystical.* Baltimore, Md. The Johns Hopkins Press, 1966.

Hederer, Edgar. *Mystik und Lyrik.* Munich: Verlag von R. Oldenbourg, 1941.

Heer, Friedrich. *The Medieval World.* Translated by Janet Sondheimer. New York and Toronto: Mentor Books and The New American Library, 1962.

Hopkins, Arthur John. *Alchemy, Child of Greek Philosophy.* New York: Columbia University Press, 1934.

James, William. *The Varieties of Religious Experience. A Study in Human Nature, being the Gifford lectures on natural religion delivered at Edinburgh in 1901–1902.* Reprint. London and New York: Longmans, Green and Co., 1935.

Jobes, Gertrude. *Dictionary of Mythology, Folklore and Symbols.* New York: The Scarecrow Press, Inc., 1961.

Jung, Carl Gustav. *The Integration of the Personality.* Translated by Stanley M. Dell. London: Routledge & K. Paul, 1950.

――――. *The Psychology of the Unconscious.* Translated by Beatrice M. Hinkle. New York: Moffat, Yard and Company, 1949.

Kayser, Rudolf. "Minne und Mystik im Werke Mechthilds von Magdeburg." *The Germanic Review* 19 (1944): 3–15.

Keen, Maurice. *A History of Medieval Europe.* New York: Frederick A. Praeger, Inc., 1968.

Kemp-Welch, Alice. "Mechthild of Magdeburg." In *Of Six Medieval Women*. London: Macmillan and Co. Ltd., 1913.

Knowles, David. *The Evolution of Medieval Thought*. New York: Vintage Books and Random House, 1962.

Kraus, Carl von, ed. *Des Minnesangs Frühling*. 34th ed. Stuttgart: S. Hirzel Verlag, 1967.

Kuhn, Hugo. *Dichtung und Welt im Mittelalter*. Stuttgart: J. B. Metzler, 1959.

Lacroix, Paul. *Science and Literature in the Middle Ages and the Renaissance*. Reprint. New York: Frederick Ungar Publishing Co., 1964.

Laski, Marghanita. *Ecstasy. A Study of Some Secular and Religious Experiences*. Bloomington, Ind.: Indiana University Press, 1962.

Lovejoy, Arthur O. *The Great Chain of Being, A Study of the History of an Idea*. Cambridge, Mass.: Harvard University Press, 1966.

Lüers, Grete. *Die Sprache der deutschen Mystik des Mittelalters im Werke der Mechthild von Magdeburg*. Munich: 1926. Reprint. Darmstadt: Wissenschaftliche Buchgesellschaft, 1966.

Menzies, Lucy. *The Revelations of Mechthild of Magdeburg (1210–1297) or The Flowing Light of the Godhead*. London: Longmans, Green and Co. Ltd., 1953.

Meyer, Lothar. "Studien zur geistlichen Bildsprache im Werke der Mechthild von Magdeburg." Ph.D. dissertation, Göttingen, 1951.

Mohr, Wolfgang. "Darbietungsformen der Mystik bei Mechthild von Magdeburg." In *Märchen, Mythos, Dichtung. Festschrift zum 90. Geburtstag Friedrich von der Leyens am 19. August 1963*. Edited by Hugo Kuhn and Kurt Schier. Munich: Verlag C. H. Beck, 1963.

Musurillo, Herbert. *Symbolism and the Christian Imagination*. Baltimore, Md.: Helicon Press, Inc., 1962.

Neumann, Hans. "Beiträge zur Textgeschichte des 'Fliessenden Lichts der Gottheit' und zur Lebensgeschichte Mechthilds von Magdeburg." In *Altdeutsche und Altniederländische Mystik*. Edited by Kurt Ruh. Darmstadt: Wissenschaftliche Buchgesellschaft, 1964.

————. "Mechthild von Magdeburg und die mittelniederländische Frauenmystik." In *Mediaeval German Studies presented to Frederick Norman by his Students, Colleagues and Friends on the Occasion of his Retirement*. Edited by A. T. Thomas and M. O'C. Walshe. London: The Institute of Germanic Studies, 1965.

————. "Problemata Mechtildiana." *Zeitschrift für deutsches Altertum und deutsche Literatur* 82 (1948/50): 143–72.

New Catholic Edition of the Holy Bible. New York: Catholic Book Publishing Company, 1954.

Ober, Peter. "Sense Images for Noetic Experience in the Works of Meister Eckhart." Ph.D. dissertation, University of California at Berkeley, 1968.

O'Brien, Elmer, ed. and trans. *The Essential Plotinus*. New York: Mentor Books and The New American Library, 1964.

Oppel, Arnold. *Das Hohelied Salomonis und die religiöse Liebeslyrik*. Vol. 32 of *Abhandlungen zur mittleren und neueren Geschichte*. Berlin: W. Rothschild Verlag, 1911.

Pickering, Frederick P. *Literature and Art in the Middle Ages*. Coral Gables, Fl.: University of Miami Press, 1970.

Piper, Paul. *Die geistliche Dichtung des Mittelalters*. 2 vols. Berlin: Verlag von W. Spemann, 1888.

Preger, Wilhelm. *Geschichte der deutschen Mystik bis zum Tode Meister Eckharts*. Vol. 1 of *Geschichte der deutschen Mystik im Mittelalter, nach den Quellen untersucht und dargestellt*. Reprint. Aalen: Otto Zeller Verlagsbuchhandlung, 1962.

Quint, Josef. "Mystik und Sprache." *Deutsche Vierteljahrsschrift für Literaturwissenschaft und Geistesgeschichte* 27 (1953): 48–76.

Rand, Edward Kennard. *Founders of the Middle Ages*. Cambridge, Mass.: Harvard University Press, 1928.

Read, John. *Prelude to Chemistry. An Outline of Alchemy*. Cambridge, Mass.: The M. I. T. Press, 1961.

Richstätter, Karl. *Die Herz-Jesu-Verehrung des deutschen Mittelalters*, 2d ed. Munich: J. Kosel and F. Dustet, 1924.

Ruh, Kurt. "Die trinitarische Spekulation in deutscher Mystik und Scholastik." *Zeitschrift für deutsche Philologie* 72 (1953): 24–53.

Sambursky, Samuel. *The Physical World of the Greeks.* Translated by Merton Dagut. New York: The Macmillan Company, 1956.

Schmidt, Margot. "Studien zum Leidproblem bei Mechthild von Magdeburg." Ph.D. dissertation, Freiburg i. Br., 1952.

Schnackenburg, Rudolf. *Baptism in the Thought of Saint Paul. A Study in Pauline Theology.* Translated by G. R. Beasley-Murray. New York: Herder and Herder, 1964.

Schneider, Hermann. *Heldendichtung, Geistlichendichtung, Ritterdichtung.* Vol. 1 of *Geschichte der deutschen Literatur.* Heidelberg: Carl Winters Universitätsbuchhandlung, 1925.

Schulze-Maizier, Friedrich, ed. *Mystiche Dichtung aus sieben Jahrhunderten.* With an introduction by F. Schulze-Maizier. Leipzig: Insel-Verlag, 1925.

Schweitzer, Albert. *The Mysticism of Paul the Apostle.* Translated by William Montgomery. New York: The Seabury Press, 1968.

Schwietering, Julius. *Die deutsche Dichtung des Mittelalters.* Potsdam: Akademische Verlagsgesellschaft Athenaion, 1940.

———. *Mystik und Höfische Dichtung im Hochmittelalter.* Darmstadt: Wissenschaftliche Buchgesellschaft, 1962.

Silberer, Herbert. *Probleme der Mystik und ihrer Symbolik.* Vienna: Heller Verlag, 1914.

Singer, Charles. "The Visions of Hildegard von Bingen." In *From Magic to Science.* New York: Boni and Liveright, 1928.

Singer, Samuel. *Die religiöse Lyrik des Mittelalters. Das Nachleben der Psalmen.* Bern: Verlag A. Francke, 1933.

Soeteman, Cornelis. *Deutsche geistliche Dichtung des 11. und 12. Jahrhunderts.* Stuttgart: J. B. Metzler, 1963.

Solmsen, Friedrich. *Aristotle's System of the Physical World: A Comparison with his Predecessors.* Ithaca, N.Y.: Cornell University Press, 1960.

Smalley, Beryl. *The Study of the Bible in the Middle Ages.* 2d ed. New York: Philosophical Library, 1952.

Stammler, Wolfgang. *Von der Mystik zum Barock 1400–1600.* Stuttgart: J. B. Metzler, 1927.

———. *Wort und Bild; Studien zu den Wechselbeziehungen zwischen Schrifttum und Bildkunst im Mittelalter.* Berlin: E. Schmidt Verlag, 1962.

———. and Langosch, Karl, eds. *Die deutsche Literatur des Mittelalters. Verfasserlexikon.* 5 vols. Berlin: Walter de Gruyter & Co., 1933–1955.

Stierling, Hubert. "Studien zu Mechthild von Magdeburg." Ph.D. dissertation, Göttingen, 1907.

Taton, René, ed. *Ancient and Medieval Science.* Vol. 1 of *History of Science.* Translated by A. J. Pomerans. New York: Basic Books, Inc., 1963.

Thorndike, Lynn. "Hildegard von Bingen." In *A History of Magic and Experimental Science, During the First Thirteen Centuries of our Era.* Vol. 2. New York: The Macmillan Company, 1923.

Tillman, Hans. "Studien zum Dialog bei Mechthild von Magdeburg." Ph.D. dissertation, Marburg, 1933.

Underhill, Evelyn. *The Essentials of Mysticism.* New York: E. P. Dutton & Co., 1920.

———. *Mysticism, A Study in the Nature and Development of Man's Spiritual Consciousness.* 3d ed. New York: E. P. Dutton and Company, 1912.

Walshe, M. O'C. *Medieval German Literature. A Survey.* Cambridge, Mass.: Harvard University Press, 1962.

Wentzlaff - Eggebert, Friedrich - Wilhelm. *Deutsche Mystik zwischen Mittelalter und Neuzeit; Einheit und Wandlung ihrer Erscheinungsformen.* 2d ed. Berlin: Walter de Gruyter & Co., 1947.

————. "Erscheinungsformen der *unio mystica* in der deutschen Literatur und Dichtung." *Deutsche Vierteljahrsschrift für Literaturwissenschaft und Geistesgeschichte* 22 (1944): 237–77.

Young, Robert. *Analytical Concordance to the Bible.* 22d American ed. Revised by William B. Stevenson. New York: Funk & Wagnalls Company, 1955.

Zinter, Edith. *Zur mystischen Stilkunst Mechthilds von Magdeburg.* Borna-Leipzig: Universitätsverlag von Robert Noske, 1931.

Index

180